BBC MUSIC GUIDES

MOZART SERENADES, DIVERTIMENTI AND DANCES

Bach Cantatas J. A. WESTRUP
Bach Organ Music PETER WILLIAMS
Bartók Chamber Music STEPHEN WALSH
Bartók Orchestral Music JOHN MCCABE
Beethoven Concertos and Overtures ROGER FISKE
Beethoven Piano Sonatas DENIS MATTHEWS
Beethoven String Quartets BASIL LAM
Beethoven Symphonies ROBERT SIMPSON
Berlioz Orchestral Music HUGH MACDONALD
Brahms Chamber Music IVOR KEYS
Brahms Piano Music DENIS MATTHEWS
Brahms Orchestral Music JOHN HORTON
Brahms Songs ERIC SAMS
Bruckner Symphonies PHILIP BARFORD
Couperin DAVID TUNLEY
Debussy Orchestral Music DAVID COX
Debussy Piano Music FRANK DAWES
Dvořák Symphonies and Concertos ROBERT LAYTON
Elgar Orchestral Music MICHAEL KENNEDY
Falla RONALD CRICHTON
Handel Concertos STANLEY SADIE
Haydn String Quartets ROSEMARY HUGHES
Haydn Symphonies H. C. ROBBINS LANDON
Mahler Symphonies and Songs PHILIP BARFORD
Mendelssohn Chamber Music JOHN HORTON
Monteverdi Church Music DENIS ARNOLD
Monteverdi Madrigals DENIS ARNOLD
Mozart Chamber Music A. HYATT KING
Mozart Piano Concertos PHILIP RADCLIFFE
Mozart Wind and String Concertos A. HYATT KING
Purcell ARTHUR HUTCHINGS
Rachmaninov Orchestral Music PATRICK PIGGOTT
Ravel Orchestral Music LAURENCE DAVIES
Schoenberg Chamber Music ARNOLD WHITTALL
Schubert Chamber Music J. A. WESTRUP
Schubert Piano Sonatas PHILIP RADCLIFFE
Schubert Songs MAURICE J. E. BROWN
Schubert Symphonies MAURICE J. E. BROWN
Schumann Orchestral Music HANS GAL
Schumann Piano Music JOAN CHISSELL
Schumann Songs ASTRA DESMOND
Shostakovich Symphonies HUGH OTTAWAY
Tchaikovsky Ballet Music JOHN WARRACK
Tchaikovsky Symphonies and Concertos JOHN WARRACK
The Trio Sonata CHRISTOPHER HOGWOOD
Vaughan Williams Symphonies HUGH OTTAWAY
Vivaldi MICHAEL TALBOT
Hugo Wolf Songs MOSCO CARNER

BBC MUSIC GUIDES

Mozart Serenades, Divertimenti and Dances

ERIK SMITH

BRITISH BROADCASTING CORPORATION

Published by the
British Broadcasting Corporation
35 Marylebone High Street
London W1M 4AA

ISBN 0 563 12862 3

First published 1982

Filmset in Great Britain by
August Filmsetting, Warrington, Cheshire
Printed in England by
Hollen Street Press, Slough, Berkshire

Contents

A Dance at Don Giovanni's

Don Giovanni, if not exactly a model in every other respect, does show us the uses to which an eighteenth-century gentleman put the occasional music of various kinds which forms the subject of this book. By providing him with three dance bands to play at his ball, Mozart lets us hear simultaneously the three kinds of dances which he composed literally by the dozen: the minuet, the German dance (*Deutsche* or *Ländler*) and the contredanse:

Ex.1 K.527

In so doing he demonstrates the relative speeds of the dances, though one should not take these as invariable, and even their social status – the noble Donna Anna and Don Ottavio dance the minuet, Leporello and Masetto the 'Deutsche', while Don Giovanni whirls Zerlina into a contredanse as a compromise between aristocratic and peasant music. The serenade with which the Don softly woos Donna Elvira's maid is, of course, quite different from the serenades described in this book, for these are instrumental and for the whole town to hear. But the wind band, playing selections from popular operas during supper, gives an exact picture of 'Tafelmusik' as it was played in the household of anybody with enough money and taste. *Figaro* too has its dance, and *Così fan tutte* its serenade, further clues to the integrated nature of Mozart's entire output: the rhythms of the dance underline most of his music, and the dramatic characterisation and passionate melody of the operas are the soul of his instrumental music. In all genres his almost instinctive craftsmanship makes a masterpiece of the smallest work.

Since this book covers far more music than most of the others in the series, it will not always be possible to linger over details, nor to include fragmentary compositions. But we must at least glance at chronology and authenticity, for there is a good deal of ground to be cleared here. As with the attribution of old paintings, the more or less informed or inspired guess of one generation has become the accepted fact of the next. Ludwig Ritter von Köchel applied his training as a botanist and his love for Mozart's music to the production of the first catalogue, published in 1862, and thus acquired the well-deserved honour of appearing, at least as far as the initial of his surname goes, wherever Mozart's work is mentioned. He also brought about the publication of Breitkopf and Härtel's Complete Edition by offering a subsidy of 15,000 guilders, which was finally paid in full by his heirs. Not only Köchel, but his equally great successor Alfred Einstein (not to mention lesser men), leapt to some strange conclusions in the matter of attribution and dating. It has even been found that some of the attributions and dating in the hand of Nissen are incorrect, something of a shock since one had always put complete faith in the worthy second husband of Mozart's widow. But worse is to come! Mozart's own thematic index, started on 9 February 1784 (with K449) and continued up to the end of his life, has been shown to be unreliable, at least during its first year. It seems that Mozart did not keep the index item by item but noted the productions of several months at a time, remembering exact details as best he could. He may have forgotten some works altogether.

Where the autographs survive scientific methods have recently yielded important results. By examining the ink, it is often possible to ascertain the sequence of composition of a work – a matter of compelling fascination when observing the creative process. Renewed study of handwritings has reversed some previous attributions, especially in now assigning to Leopold Mozart a number of autographs and, more especially, of headings and tempo indications formerly thought to be in his son's own hand. Of course, Leopold may have been copying his son's rough drafts or following his instructions.

The study of watermarks in the manuscript paper has produced the most radical developments. If a sheet of paper is large enough, it is possible to discover where it was manufactured. Since Mozart tended to travel a good deal and bought new manuscript paper whenever he ran out of it, it has become possible to say where – and therefore to some extent when – a manuscript was written.

If the autograph has not survived and there are no early copies of the work or references to it, it is always tempting to study the music itself as evidence of authenticity. But this is far too subjective to be reliable. Even here, however, modern methods have been used. A computer can be fed with the statistics of the known genuine works – relative length of the various parts of a movement, symmetry or otherwise of the melodies, patterns of modulation and so on – and it will compare these with the statistics of the questionable work.

Nearly every work Mozart ever wrote was intended for some particular performance, but this is especially true of the light music which is the subject of this book. It therefore seems appropriate to place it in its setting, with some details of time and place which would have been much less relevant in a study of more absolute music.

'GALIMATHIAS MUSICUM', K32

After their three-year tour of France and England, the Mozarts found themselves in The Hague during the celebrations for the installation of Prince William of Orange as hereditary Statthalter of the Netherlands on 8 March 1766. The ten-year-old Wolfgang composed an odd pot-pourri for the occasion, described by his father as 'a quodlibet under the title of Gallimathias Musicum for two oboes, two horns, cembalo obligato, two bassoons, two violins, viola and bass. All the instruments have their solos and at the end there is a fugue with all the instruments on a Dutch song called Prince William.' Various copies and autograph sketches survive. Leopold clearly had a hand in the composition, first in the very idea of quoting Alpine folk-music in comic little numbers (his own frequent practice as in his 'Toy Symphony', 'Peasant Wedding' and 'Musical Sleigh Ride'), and secondly in contributing entire pieces of his own, like the Pastorella (No. 4), and in bringing the fugue to a successful conclusion. There are seventeen numbers in all (some only a few bars long), including a contredanse for solo harpsichord, and a chorus presumably to be sung by the instrumentalists. It is all very melodious and entertaining, but unambitious when we consider the fine First Symphony composed the previous year.

Throughout his life Mozart found melodic inspiration, especially for his dances and divertimenti, in the folk-music of Austria and Swabia (his father's homeland) and later of Bohemia. But he kept notably aloof from the effects and jokes in which Leopold found it necessary to indulge. The figure of the young composer in the Prologue of the Strauss–Hofmannsthal *Ariadne auf Naxos* was inspired by the child Mozart; remember how he protests against the exigencies of the entertainment industry, just as Mozart might have done against having to turn out the childish Galimathias. 'Musik ist eine heilige Kunst.'

Much later Mozart did put a post-horn into a serenade, and at the end of his life he used special effects, hurdy-gurdies, sleigh-bells and post-horns in some dances. The very first work he composed after the death of his beloved father was the 'Musical Joke', K522. This was a strange time, it would seem, for jokes. But the work was much more after Leopold's heart than Wolfgang's, and it may have been composed as a pious deed. One can imagine Mozart improvising a piece to ridicule all the bad composers of the time, and Leopold, with his waspish view of his contemporaries, making him promise to write it down; and then Wolfgang remembering his unfulfilled promise too late.

Music in the Open Air

One of the most delightful features about Austria and, no doubt, other lands of temperate summer climates, was the celebration of every possible occasion by the performance of music in the open air. An English traveller wrote from Vienna in 1684 (to take one out of hundreds of examples) that a serenade was played before his window almost every evening. In Mozart's Salzburg there were two kinds of serenade. Serenades for full orchestra were for grand celebrations – the end of the university year, the Archbishop's name day or the wedding of the Bürgermeister's daughter. The divertimenti, performed by half a dozen players, were for more modest family occasions. Mozart never headed the autographs of these works, but in his letters refers to them as *Finalmusiken* or *Cassationen*. *Finalmusiken* refers to the completion of their studies by members of the Faculties of 'Logic' and of 'Physic' at Salzburg University; serenades were commissioned and organised every August in honour of the Prince Archbishop and the professors. 'Cassation' is a legal term meaning 'making null and void', but no one has been able to explain why Mozart used this title.

Leopold Mozart usually headed the autographs 'serenata' or 'serenada', but in practice all these terms were interchangeable – except that 'divertimento' was consistently used for works for one or more solo instruments. Haydn called all his early keyboard sonatas 'divertimenti'; and Mozart occasionally used the term for pieces of pure chamber music, such as the Piano Trio, K254, and the String Trio, K563. With its extra minuet and variation movement the latter has a claim to be considered a divertimento (it is fully discussed in A. Hyatt King's book in this series, *Mozart Chamber Music*). The heading 'Divertimento' on the autograph of K131, obviously an orchestral piece, is not in Mozart's hand; but it was misleadingly retained for the work until the publication of the New Complete Edition.

SERENADES, DIVERTIMENTI, CASSATIONS AND MARCHES

(Composed in Salzburg unless otherwise indicated; some dates hypothetical; the K numbers in brackets refer to the sixth edition of the catalogue, 1964)

K63	Cassation in G	Summer 1769
K99 (63a)	Cassation in B flat	Summer 1769
K100 (62 & 62a)	March and Serenade in D	Summer 1769
K113	Concerto or Divertimento in E flat (Milan)	November 1771
K136 (125a)	Divertimento in D	Early 1772
K137 (125b)	Divertimento in B flat	Early 1772
K138 (125c)	Divertimento in F	Early 1772
K131	Serenade in D	June 1772
K189 & K185 (167b & 167a)	March and Serenade in D (Vienna)	July 1773
K290 & K205 (167AB & 167A)	March and Divertimento in D	July 1773
K237 & K203 (189c & 189b)	March and Serenade in D	August 1774
K215 & K204 (213b & 213a)	March and Serenade in D	5 August 1775
K214	March in C	20 August 1775
K239	Serenata notturna in D	January 1776
K248 & K247	March and Divertimento in F	June 1776
K249 & K250 (249 & 248b)	March and 'Haffner' Serenade in D	July 1776

K251	Divertimento in D	July 1776
K286 (269a)	Notturno in D	January 1777
K287 (271H)	Divertimento in B flat	February or June 1777
K335, Nos. 1 & 2, *and* K320 (320a & 320)	2 Marches *and* 'Post-horn' Serenade in D	August 1779
K445 & 334 (320c & 320b)	March and Divertimento in D	Summer 1779
K408 No. 2 & K385 (385a & 385)	March and 'Haffner' Symphony composed as a serenade (Vienna)	July 1782
K408 Nos. 1 & 3 (383e & 383F)	2 Marches (Vienna)	1782
K522	'Ein musikalischer Spass' (Vienna)	14 June 1787
K525	'Eine kleine Nachtmusik' (Vienna)	10 August 1787

THE SERENADES FOR ORCHESTRA

Mozart's serenades are descended from the symphony, the baroque suite and the concerto. From the symphony – or Italian overture – they inherit the brilliance of the outer movements and the tenderness of the slow movements. From the baroque suite with its many dance movements come the minuets, gavottes and gigues (Mozart names only the first of these). And there is nearly always a concertante element in the serenades. There was certainly a south German tradition of long serenades with solos, as is shown by Leopold's letters and by certain works by Michael Haydn (Joseph's younger brother and Second Kappellmeister in Salzburg). But it was Mozart himself who, during the decade from 1769 to 1779, developed the form from modest beginnings to the great works we shall examine below.

How do the serenades differ from the symphonies written at the same time? The symphonies consist of two *allegros*, with a slow movement and usually a minuet in between. The serenades also have two *allegros*, but sometimes with slow introductions (to the first and last movements), and sometimes with a change of tempo or time in the finale. There are two slow movements – one usually a soulful *adagio*, the other a slow gavotte or march – and two minuets, sometimes with several trios. In addition there is usually the concertante section in place of one of the slow movements, normally a violin concerto consisting of another *andante*, minuet and *allegro*. The musicians arrived and departed playing the music of a specially-composed march.

Except for the first two, K63 and K99, all these works are in D major, a key suitable to the festive trumpets and more brilliant for the string instruments than C major, the other key in which trumpets were normally played. On the whole, the serenades are fully the equal of the other symphonic works of the period (except for those great masterpieces, the early G minor and A major symphonies) and perhaps their superior in melodic invention. In 1781 Mozart wrote to his father that he had really taken trouble with the composition of his great Wind Serenade in E flat (K375), because it was to be heard by a man influential at court. Mozart certainly took pains with his serenades, for he knew that half the population of Salzburg would come to hear them.

The trouble is that because of their leisurely character and rather static harmony the serenades make better listening in the open on a summer's evening than in a modern concert hall. And so we hear this delightful music far too rarely. When Mozart himself used the music of his serenades for subsequent concert performances, he played only the four movements that make up the symphony; or he would play only the concertante movements. (Mozart writes of playing the 'sinfonia concertante' from K320 in a Vienna concert in 1783.)

We can get a clear picture of an evening's musical entertainment in Salzburg from the following reports. One is from the diary of Wolfgang's sister Nannerl in August 1775: 'The *Finalmusik* took place on the 9th. It left our house at half past eight, played in the Mirabell until a quarter to ten, and thence to the Colegio where it lasted until after eleven.' (Since each serenade takes the best part of an hour, and the Mirabell – the Archbishop's town residence – was about fifteen minutes' walk from the university across the river, we learn that the two performances took place without interruption.) And Leopold, writing to his son in June 1778, says:

The day after tomorrow is the feast of St Anthony and you're not there. Who is to arrange a serenade for the Countess? Who? Why, La Compagnie des Amateurs. Count Czernin and Kolb are the two *violini principali* with astonishing solos. The composition is the Allegro and Adagio by Hafeneder, the Minuet with three Trios by Czernin (NB all specially composed), the March by Hafeneder, but it's all bad stolen stuff.... Cavaliers and court officials all walk along with the march, all except for me, because I am unlucky enough to have lost my memory for learning music by heart!

The march was therefore played en route by heart, and the whole serenade was played standing. For this reason cellos and timpani (and of course keyboard continuo) were not included. The bass line was taken by bassoons and small double-basses which could be strapped to the players and, with some discomfort, actually played on the march. Leopold's next report, amusingly malicious, gives us more of the social background to this music:

I wrote to you about Czernin's Serenade: it had a sad, ridiculous, asinine result. Czernin wanted to perform it on the same evening to the Countess Lodron and to his own sister. Now, his first idiocy was to play first to his sister and then to the Countess, not only because the wife of a Landmarschall takes precedence by far over the wife of a Schlossoberst but because his sister, the Countess Lizow, with her innate modesty would gladly have left the honour of the first serenade to a lady not related to them. But his second idiocy was even more incomprehensible. When the music had begun outside Countess Lodron's house, Czernin looked up at the windows and kept shouting. Then came the minuet and trio, only once, then an adagio which he worked very hard to play appallingly badly, while he kept speaking to the concert master, Brunetti, who stood behind him, and shouting out aloud. And then 'allons! marche!' and went off with the band in an instant, as one might do if one intended to offer somebody a public insult with a serenade, for half the town was present. And why? Because he imagined that the Countess had not come to the window, in which impression Brunetti confirmed him, although the Countess with Prince Breiner were seen at the window by everybody else. A couple of days later the Countess, meeting him in company, gave Brunetti a terrible telling-off, and since then the Archbishop will not speak to him!

These letters vividly portray not only the serenade evenings, but also Mozart's life in Salzburg: the tittle-tattle and small scandals observed by half the town, the band playing before a noble house and then marching off at a word of command, the generally low standards of composition and performance.

Writing to his sister from Italy in August 1770, on his way to the composition and production of his first opera seria, *Mitridate*, the fourteen-year-old Mozart listed the opening bars of 'various cassations' – the three now numbered K63, K99 and K100. Two of them must have been *Finalmusiken* performed within a few days of each other in August 1769 for the celebrations of the physicians and logicians, while the third must have at least been composed before the departure for Italy in December 1769.

K63 Cassation in G

Marche; 1 *Allegro*; 2 *Andante*; 3 Menuet; 4 *Adagio*; 5 Menuet; 6 Finale; *Allegro assai*

The headings, with the French spellings 'marche' and 'menuet' are in Leopold's hand. The two oboes and two horns are not essential, since they provide little more than doubling or harmony, but they add to the thrill of the sound, especially in the march and finale. The march (except that it has little melodic interest) is something of a prototype for those that are to follow until an older and more inventive Mozart abandons this strict baroque symmetry. The opening of the second part in the relative minor, followed by the same four-bar phrase in the dominant and then a modified re-capitulation, represents the pattern of many of Mozart's marches. The *allegro* has more rhythmic than melodic vitality, some exciting antiphonal effects between first and second violins add a general feeling of violin bravura, especially in the jumps from the heights to the depths, so common in Mozart's violin (and vocal) writing:

Ex.2

Since wind instruments at this stage have little to contribute but a merry noise, they are omitted from both slow movements. The *andante* is a slow march with muted violins and mostly pizzicato lower strings; there is a chromatic hint at the minor, which gives the return to C major a special serenity. The *adagio* consists of a long, eloquent, richly decorated violin solo, making no great technical demands on the player, but perfectly written all up and down the instrument. It is Mozart's first violin solo. There is an exceptionally rich accompaniment of a type that returns in other serenades, an impression of the murmurs of a summer evening – violins muted and in different rhythms, violas *divisi*, and the bass in yet another slower rhythmic pattern of its own. In the first 'menuet' the top and bottom line are in canon at one bar's distance, not quite rigorously throughout, for at a certain point the bass ceases to follow and takes the lead instead. The other 'menuet', in an infectiously jaunty rhythm, is chiefly notable for the characteristic addition of two bars, or rather one bar repeated, to avoid the excessive symmetry of a minuet's four- or eight-bar phrases. The finale is a short rondo on a hunting theme.

K99 Cassation in B flat

Marche; 1 *Allegro*; 2 *Andante*; 3 Menuet; 4 *Andante*; 5 Menuet; 6 Finale
This is altogether a gentler, more intimate work than the other two

cassations. It might even have been intended for performance by solo string instruments, like the divertimenti. The march is much more thoughtful than that of K63 – the chromatic viola part of the first two bars would be enough to establish that. Only the *allegro molto* has that constant brisk motion and superficial brilliance with contrasting *forte* and *piano* sections, which marks the transition from contrapuntal baroque writing to the dynamic early classical style. The first *andante*, without wind, has a touchingly simple violin melody (not headed 'solo' as in K63) with murmuring second violin and viola, all these muted, and with pizzicato bass. But the second *andante* is one of those surprising pieces of early Mozart which remain virtually without parallel: the key of G minor, the use of the two oboes occasionally to sustain a note, occasionally to rise above the violins, the combination of simple counterpoint and sweet intervals, the poignant suspensions near the end – all these give an impression of a sinfonia from one of J. S. Bach's more pastoral cantatas.

The first minuet has a formal canonic opening and an expressive trio, the second is more of the *Ländler* variety with an implied one-in-the-bar rhythm. The finale resembles nothing so much as one of Scarlatti's sonatas (though Mozart could hardly have known them any more than he would Bach's cantatas at this stage), for each section has a brisk *allegro*, with more than a feel of the harpsichord, leading into a languid siciliana. At the end of it there are three special bars to lead back to the march.

K62 March   K100 Cassation in D

Marche: 1 *Allegro*; 2 *Andante*; 3 Menuet; 4 *Allegro*; 5 Menuet; 6 *Andante*; 7 Menuet; 8 *Allegro*

As far as the first and the last four movements are concerned, this cassation follows the lines of the previous two – a brisk exuberant opening *allegro*, two minuets, a suave *andante* (in which flutes take the place of the oboes – eighteenth-century wind players were usually required to be able to play both, so this change of instruments for one movement is not uncommon), a finale identical in shape to that of K63. But we also find for the first time a built-in sinfonia concertante, the soloists being an oboe and a horn. Their roles in the second and fourth movements and the trio of the third create a landmark in Mozart's writing, not only because they consist of real *obbligato* parts with a pause for a duet cadenza in each part of the *andante*, while the strings are relegated to the accompaniment, but because the horn part goes far beyond the natural harmonics, in a manner very exceptional indeed at this date. But more of this when we come to the Serenade in D, K131.

K131 'Divertimento' or Serenade in D

1 *Allegro*; 2 *Adagio*; 3 Menuetto with three trios; 4 *Allegretto*; 5 Menuetto with two trios; 6 *Adagio–allegro molto–allegro assai*

A special word must at once be said about the remarkable writing for the four horns in this work, which remained unique for half a century or more. Until the invention of the valve-horn in the nineteenth-century, the notes of the horn, as of the trumpet, were confined to the natural harmonics of the instrument. Mozart normally only used the following ten notes:

Ex.3

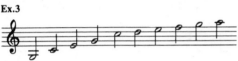

Only by changing the crook could a new set of harmonics be introduced, the crook required by the composer usually correspond-ing to the key of the piece. By inserting the right hand into the bell of the horn a skilled player could, however, modify the pitch of the note he was producing with his lips, and actually play a chromatic scale. The Salzburg horn player, Ignaz Leutgeb, was a very skilful player indeed: Mozart wrote his horn concertos and horn duos for him, and it is likely that he played the first horn parts in the original performance of K100 and K131. Mozart uses this technique in the Wind Serenades, K375 and K388 (but not K361), in the Quintet, K452, in the Divertimento, K252, and in one aria in *Idomeneo*, but he only very rarely calls for this skill in the orchestral music. Where he uses four horns, as he did in 1772–3, or two horns and two trumpets, it is to have one pair of instruments in the tonic, the other in the dominant or relative major, in order to make more of the natural notes available.

But in K131 (June 1772) Mozart suddenly writes all four horn parts as though there were no limitations to the instrument at all. The four between them are required to play twenty out of the twenty-six semitones from the (sounding) G sharp at the bottom of the bass clef, producing a richness of horn melody akin to that of the Concertos, and the romantic part-writing of the introduction to the finale:

Ex.4

Leutgeb may have played first horn, but who were the other three? Were they travelling Bohemian virtuosi? Or was it all an over-ambitious attempt, on the part of Mozart and the horn-players, to impress the new Archbishop, for whose installation the work was probably written? If so, it might have been the start of Mozart's disastrous relationship with him! Imagine the horn parts played by less than the greatest players of the day, remembering that the parts are quite difficult even on modern valve instruments. Mozart certainly never attempted anything remotely like this again, and even the four skilled players required for the Serenade K 361 never have to depart from the natural tones of the horn.

Apart from these horns, which rest during the second and fourth

Ex. 4 (cont.)

movements and in some of the trios, there are an oboe, a bassoon and a flute which has an important and brilliant solo part. And the strings make a greater melodic contribution than they do in the concertante movements of K100. The witty, march-like *allegretto* is a delight, and in the *adagio* we meet another of Mozart's long violin cantilenas. The last surprise he has in store for us is the change of tempo in the finale, when we are unexpectedly whirled off in a lively

Ländler by way of a coda. We ought to hear K131 far more often than we do, for it is full of invention and not over long.

K189 March   K185 Serenade (Andretter)

1 *Allegro assai*; 2 *Andante*; 3 *Allegro*; 4 Menuetto; 5 *Andante grazioso*; 6 Menuetto and two trios; 7 *Adagio*; 8 *Allegro assai*

This serenade was performed as a *Finalmusik* in Salzburg in August 1773. The reference to an 'Andretter serenade' in a letter of Leopold's has led to the name of this family being connected with K185, probably because J. T. von Andretter graduated in 1773 and was responsible for the commission to Mozart, who was on a visit to Vienna and had to work there.

This is another grand work with two horns and trumpets, and flutes alternating with oboes. The march has a second subject with a splendidly swinging gait, while the 'symphonic' movements have all the brilliance we have come to expect. The first movement constantly repeats its motto, which is obviously some sort of a joke. Einstein, who mistakenly supposed the serenade to have been written for a wedding celebration, found a saucy innuendo in this phrase. The finale is another rousing gallop with hunting horns, but it is introduced by a short, though very romantic, *adagio*. The second, third, and sixth movements (in the menuetto movements, the solo violin always plays in the trio only) form Mozart's First Violin Concerto. Its *andante* is a touching, simple aria: in fact the slow movements of these concertos are almost identical in form and content with the operatic arias of the time. Here, for example, the second subject is introduced by a long note held by the violin above the rest of the orchestra, an effect used a thousand times from the early Neapolitan operas onwards, through Handel to Mozart's own arias and violin concerto *andante*s (for example, K203, and K204). This type of introduction always has great beauty, but never more so than in the entry of the solo instruments in the first movement of the Sinfonia Concertante, K364. This early concerto is not of that calibre, and the *allegro* with its jolly theme and rather mechanical triplet figurations for the soloist hardly gives us cause to expect the violin concertos that were to follow during the next two and a half years.

K237 March   K203 Serenade (Colloredo) in D

1 *Andante maestoso – allegro assai*; 2 *Andante*; 3 Menuetto; 4 *Allegro*; 5 Menuetto; 6 *Andante*; 7 Menuetto; 8 *Prestissimo*

The autograph bears the words 'Serenata del Sgr. Wolfgang Amadeo Mozart, nel mese d'agosto 1774'. The date is firmly crossed out, but it now seems more probable than that suggested by Mozart's first biographer, Niemetschek. He believed that the serenade was written for Archbishop Hieronymus Colloredo's name-day, which fell on 30 September. In fact, K203 is probably a *Finalmusik* like the majority of the serenades – but the name 'Colloredo' has stuck. The Violin Concerto in B flat, which forms the second, third and fourth movements, is much finer than that of the previous year. The *andante* has a stream of melody, one phrase following another with that inevitability, as of a plant growing, of which Mozart unconsciously possessed the secret. There are many inventive touches, such as the oboes' comment in the second bar (Einstein compared it to opera buffa patter under a lyrical line, but it is even closer to the cackle of geese). The *allegro* has great élan, and one can observe the eighteen-year-old composer learning and revealing more of the violin's possibilities in each work. The minuet and trio each have an *ostinato* joke.

In the remaining movements, though there are also flutes, horns and trumpets, it is the first oboe which is singled out, especially in a wonderful D minor trio and for its role in the muted murmuring *andante*. (It was of course K203, minus the Violin Concerto, which was performed in 1778 – as mentioned by Leopold: 'your *Finalmusik* Symphonie, *andante* and trio with oboe solo' – and not K251 as is usually claimed.) The opening *allegro*, with a fine *andante maestoso* introduction (the beginning of which echoes the march) and the final *prestissimo* give us the busy bravura and lilting melodies that we have come to expect in these works.

K215 March   K204 Serenade

1 *Allegro assai*; 2 *Andante moderato*; 3 *Allegro*; 4 Menuetto; 5 *Andante*; 6 Menuetto; 7 *Andante grazioso*; 8 *Allegro*

Composed a year later than K203, for the same occasion, K204 contains an even finer Violin Concerto in A major in the second, third and fourth movements. This is not surprising, for K204 was composed between the second and third of his famous Violin Concertos. The march has the festive spring of many another, and

Mozart was to remember it in the *Tito* march sixteen years later. The seventh movement, based on a melody Mozart used again and again in his earlier works, has a concertante part for flute, oboe, bassoon and two horns (who are required to play some notes beyond the natural harmonics, but by no means in the hair-raising manner of K131).

The finale is a delightfully inventive and amusing double rondo: a slow march stumbles along with various hesitations and falls into the arms of a fiery 3/8 *allegro*, but returns three more times in various guises to suffer the same fate. The first oboe has an important part to play.

K239 Serenata notturna

1 *Marcia maestoso*; 2 Menuetto; 3 Rondeau, *allegretto*

There is an autograph dating, January 1776, from which, together with the presence of timpani, we can deduce that K239 was written for indoor performance. Mozart uses the baroque concerto grosso in an entirely new way: his concertino is the basic divertimento ensemble, two violins, viola and double-bass, leaving the violins, violas, cellos and timpani to the ripieno orchestra. Why only cellos? Perhaps only one double-bass was available: but either the timpani or the concertino bass are always on hand to double the ripieno cello. This is another work of almost magical grace and elegance, with a folk-tune and a mock recitative to enliven the finale.

K250 'Haffner' Serenade

1 *Allegro maestoso – allegro molto*; 2 *Andante*; 3 Menuetto; 4 Rondeau; 5 Menuetto galante; 6 *Andante*; 7 Menuetto with two trios; 8 *Adagio – allegro assai*

Composed for the wedding of the daughter of Salzburg's Bürgermeister, Siegmund Haffner, on 22 July 1776, this is Mozart's longest instrumental work, for it lasts about an hour (with all the repeats) and epitomises both the charm and the weakness of the serenades. It shows Mozart in an unusually prolix mood, especially in the rather formal and empty opening *allegro maestoso*. There is a great deal of merry noise of oboes, trumpets and shimmering violins with some good tunes – just what the Bürgermeister ordered and most exhilarating when taken with champagne. In the more staid circumstances of orchestral concerts nowadays, it would perhaps be better to play only the movements that make up the Symphony (one, two and eight with one or two minuets) as Mozart certainly did; and on another occasion the Violin concerto.

The first movement is carefully constructed:

Ex.5

The figure (Ex. 5) which appears in the first bar later provides the rhythmical impetus for the development section and also ends the movement. The other two melodic fragments (Ex. 6a and b) that make up the introduction are also used in the *allegro molto*, a very rare instance of musical material shared between a movement and its introduction:

Ex.6

(a)

(b)

The development section consists of six repeats of a four-bar phrase in various keys, an academic procedure which Mozart usually left to his lesser contemporaries. In the otherwise magnificent Violin Sonata in D major, K306, however, he actually repeats a two-bar phrase twelve times in a circle of modulating keys.

The second to fourth movements form the Violin Concerto, undoubtedly originally performed by Mozart himself. The *andante* is full of expressive melody – too full, one might almost add, in consideration of the no less beautiful but certainly less expansive slow movements of the violin concertos written six months before. The third movement is a minuet in G minor: since it bears some melodic resemblance to the minuet of the Symphony in G minor, K550, it is interesting to consider the similarities and the essential differences which make the Symphony's minuet passionate and tragic, while the other remains merely elegantly melancholy. Melodically the similarities are striking, both in the openings (Ex. 7) and in the chromatic passage which leads to the dominant, but K250 has the chromatic scale in the bass and K550 in the violins (Ex. 8).

Ex.7
(a) K.250

(b) K.550

Ex.8
(a) K.250

(b) K.550

The essential difference lies in the rhythm: K250 is made up of four-bar phrases which neatly balance each other. K550 has two three-bar phrases followed by two four-bar phrases in the first section; more important still is the syncopated accent on the third beat, which persists throughout the movement in the top and bottom lines, except where a melodic accent makes itself felt on the second beat with an even greater effect of urgency. The whole expression in K550 is one of nervous striving with, at last, hopeless resignation in the concluding *piano* bars which end the minuet of the Serenade. This contrasts with the confident repetition of the opening four bars. The contrasting G major of the trio is a special delight in each case, but one could not pretend that the perky tune played by the solo violin in the Serenade even began to match 'What the angels sing' in K550, as Schubert described it. But, if we keep a clear head about the difference between delightful music and very great music (as not all lovers of the eighteenth century do) that is not to denigrate one of the best movements of this period. Schubert must have liked it, for in his Second and Fifth Symphonies, both in the major, he used minuets in the minor, that of his Fifth Symphony being very similar to K250.

The fourth movement, a full sonata rondo plus two extra episodes, has a comic subject which also supplies much of the material for the rest of the movement. The soloist's almost obsessive fiddling is ever mocked by the horns. The fifth and seventh movements are minuets. As usual, one is of the stately old-fashioned sort with three beats in the bar: in fact the fifth movement is actually marked *menuetto galante*, to indicate this. Sometimes Mozart wrote *menuetto grazioso* or *menuetto allegretto* (as in the Post-horn Serenade) or *tempo di menuetto* for the same purpose, but usually the character and tempo of the dance must be determined by the performer from the music alone. This fifth movement is a counterpart to the third. The perky dotted rhythm of the major mode trio of the third movement characterises this D major minuet; and now the trio is in the minor, with a marvellous characteristic use of divided violas. The seventh movement is clearly a minuet of the brisk *Ländler* variety, a close relation to some of the *Deutsche* of 1790–1. The second trio has an amusing 'toy trumpet' effect.

The sixth movement is the richest melodically and formally the most complex. It is not altogether successful, however. Considering that Mozart had already achieved the sheer perfection of the Symphony in A major, K201, and the Violin Concerto in A major, K219, this *andante* is a somewhat sprawling affair. Equipped with the formal apparatus to create, say, a four-minute movement, Mozart was suddenly faced with the task of composing one twice as long (for an hour's music had been ordered). Although the character of some of the melodies puts us in mind of Schubert, Mozart's 'heavenly length' was made up in quite a different way. It is worthwhile analysing the structure of this movement, because Mozart seems to have had to strive to create the form he needed and, for once, did not really succeed. In the great piano concertos he did build a new wider structure on the basis of sonata or rondo form with complete success. But in this *andante* he seems to have thrown away the strong polarities of key, which form the basis of classical form, and returned to something like the loose rondo form of the baroque movement where the tonic is rarely absent for long.

The main subjects are:

Ex. 9   A

This always comes in the tonic with a repeat and on each occasion a variation:

Ex. 10   B

This is also always in the tonic and always repeated but without any variation, and:

Ex. 11   C

Though this would seem to be the second subject we have been waiting for, it makes its appearance in the tonic, followed by a phrase of great eloquence, and finally the awaited modulation to the dominant over a demisemiquaver murmur, which could be derived from Ex. 10. The second subject in E major proves to be none other than Ex. 11 in a chromatic version played by the oboe. A coda (Ex. 12) predictably concludes the first part.

Ex. 12   D

Apart from this short section in the dominant and the eloquent F sharp minor melody that follows (Ex. 13), all the rest of the movement is in the tonic key. Below Ex. 13 is a diagram of the structure of this multiple rondo; the keys are given in the second line.

Ex. 13 E

```
A B C c D    B E A c D    B C A B C
A A A E E    A F A A A    A A A A A
```

These are beautiful tunes with ever-inventive variations, but one suspects that Mozart himself was dissatisfied with the harmonic monotony of this long movement, for we meet nothing like it again.

In the *adagio* introduction to the eighth movement, we find all the expressive eloquence we missed at the beginning of the serenade. In fact, these sixteen bars would not be out of place in one of the later works and even recall, at least in character, the introduction to the *Prague* Symphony. In the *allegro assai* all is exuberance and breathless excitement, with a happy second subject and an extra new one after the double-bar (new, that is, in K250, but one very like it had already put in an appearance in the finale of the Violin Concerto in G major, K216, and at the beginning of the String Quartet, K156). The impetus never lets up, except for a brief fermata before the concluding bars. The wedding guests must have cheered.

In 1785 Mozart hurriedly composed another D major Serenade for a Haffner festivity. By subsequently removing the march and the second minuet, he placed it amongst his symphonies (K385).

K286 Notturno for four orchestras

1 *Andante*; 2 *Allegretto grazioso*; 3 Menuetto

The autograph, now lost, is headed in an unknown hand 'Notturno from the last years of the 1770s'. It is assumed to have been written a year after K239 and for a similar occasion. But it is hard to think of an effective *indoor* setting demanded by the date, January 1777. One could imagine it performed in the Mirabell gardens, or in some other noble French-style garden, where the echoing orchestras might have been hidden behind separate hedges. Once again Mozart uses a form new to him but which has an honourable ancestry going back in this case to the multi-choral writing of the Gabrielis in Venice.

The first orchestra plays a phrase, the last part of which is echoed by a similar orchestra a little farther off, which is echoed by a third orchestra farther still and by a fourth far away. Then the first orchestra begins with the next phrase. The effect is magical – an almost realistic echo such as one might hear in the mountains near Salzburg. Normally each orchestra echoes a shorter phrase than the preceding one, but Mozart avoids any suspicion of monotony by sometimes letting the echoes clash or cut across each other with an effect of splendid confusion:

Ex.14   K.286

Even so, by the time he had written the minuet he must have felt he had exhausted all the possibilities: the trio, added later, is for the first orchestra only. In fact each 'orchestra' probably consisted of only a sextet – two violins, viola, double-bass and two horns – for it is unlikely that there were enough musicians available to provide four orchestras with more than one player to a part.

K335 (320a) 2 marches in D   K320 'Post-horn' Serenade in D

1 *Adagio maestoso – allegro con spirito*; 2 Menuetto; 3 'Sinfonia concertante', *Andante grazioso*; 4 Rondeau *allegro ma non troppo*; 5 *Andantino*; 6 Menuetto; 7 Finale *presto*

Having examined the 'Haffner' Serenade in some detail, it is interesting to compare it with the 'Post-horn' Serenade, completed on 3 August 1779 as a university *Finalmusik*. The three years which separated the writing of these Serenades were, perhaps, the most decisive in Mozart's life. First, there were the emotional upheavals during the great journey to Munich, Mannheim and Paris which lasted from September 1777 to January 1779. He fell in love for the first time and was rejected by Aloysia Weber (whose sister he later married). In Paris he felt for the first time the bitterness of the situation of a former infant prodigy in a world which only cares for novelty. And he experienced his first personal tragedy in the death of his mother, who had accompanied him. Finally, on his return, he must have realised that Salzburg provided too small a field for his endeavours, and that he must soon rebel against the status of a liveried servant.

Yet these painful discoveries find less expression in the music of his next serenade than do the musical events of that journey – at Mannheim, which had the best orchestra in Europe, then the Paris orchestra, and the wind-playing of the quartet of musicians for whom he wrote a sinfonia concertante. He also renewed contact with Johann Christian Bach, whom he had known when he visited London as a child. These happier discoveries all left their mark on the 'Post-horn' Serenade.

The six bars of introductory *adagio maestoso* build up more tension than the equivalent thirty-five bars of the 'Haffner' Serenade. Now, too, there is a festive sound of trumpets, but there is also a nervous tension in the violins' syncopations which anticipate the *Prague* Symphony. There are long *crescendi*, rarely indicated in Mozart's music, but which were the most famous effect of the Mannheim orchestra. There is the thrilling tremor of the violins, to be found in Mozart's *Paris* Symphony:

Ex.15

Mozart used this many times again, for example in the overture to *Figaro*; and the opera buffa phrase which breaks in (in unison) when things seem to be getting too earnest:

Ex.16

The minuets (second and sixth movements) show fewer differences in character than those of K250: certainly the trios are all in the style of a *Ländler*. It is the second trio of the sixth movement which gives its name to the Serenade, for here a *corno di posta* in A fits into the music its characteristic octave call, a happy reminder perhaps to the students that term was over and they would soon be taking a post-chaise for home.

Instead of a violin concerto, K320 contains a 'concertante', *andante grazioso* and 'Rondeau', for the two flutes, two oboes and two bassoons, with strings and horns. This is uncomplicated, agreeable music, very close to J. C. Bach's Quintets Op. 11 for flute, oboe and strings, which Mozart perhaps heard or saw when he met the composer in Paris. In the end, the sweetness of the thirds and sixths does make us feel the need for contrast. Mozart must have felt it too, for his fifth movement is an intense *andantino* in D minor, by far the most deeply felt of any movement in the Salzburg serenades. Here, if anywhere, we must seek the emotional influences of the Paris journey. However, the opening subject is very close to the slow movement of the remarkable *Jeunehomme* Concerto in E flat, K271, composed before the Paris journey. This elegiac character comes up periodically in Mozart's music and to wonderful effect – for example, in the slow movement of the Sinfonia Concertante, K364, written soon after.

The finale brings a display of high spirits, but with what wealth of detail compared with the 'Haffner' Serenade! It is in the independence of the woodwind instruments that this is mostly to be sought, not in a concertante character, which had after all been admirably done in K131, but as part of the orchestra, on equal terms with the violins, linking and answering their phrases and introducing new ones of their own.

Alone among the serenades, the 'Post-horn' has an original timpani part. (There is a timpani part for the first, fifth, seventh and eighth movements of the 'Haffner' Serenade but this is in Leopold Mozart's hand, and was presumably for a later, indoor performance.) Perhaps somebody had the idea at last of setting up the kettle-drums and the player to await the arrival of the marching musicians. There is, of course, no timpani part in the two Marches which Mozart wrote for this occasion (for all the other serenades the same march had to suffice for coming and going). The first March, K335 (320a) No. 1, is a particularly delightful example of Mozart's fertile invention outstripping formal considerations (which in any case need not be too earnest in a piece on this small scale): instead of the return of the martial opening, at the recapitulation we have a new eloquent tune played *piano* by oboes and horns with an accompaniment of flowing quavers in the strings.

DIVERTIMENTI WITH SOLO STRINGS

The eighteenth century consumed a vast amount of music – commissioned, hurriedly composed, barely rehearsed, performed once and laid aside. Not only princes wanted their own special music for a festivity, but many a prosperous merchant too. This was just as well for the composers, for here was their best source of income. What were the others? Teaching, performing (usually with the risk of being their own concert promoter), selling a set of works to a publisher before they were pirated anyway, or presenting a neat dedication copy of a new work to somebody rich and then standing back in the hope of a reward – usually a watch or snuffbox, but rarely money, as Mozart complains. Otherwise one could only find permanent employment as the liveried servant of a prince – being reproved, as Haydn was, for one's laziness in composing too few symphonies!

The Salzburg Divertimenti were mostly composed to celebrate birthdays or name-days, like K251 for Mozart's sister, Nannerl, or K247 and K287 for the Countess Lodron.

K113 Divertimento in E flat for two clarinets, two horns and strings

1 *Allegro*; 2 *Andante*; 3 Menuetto; 4 *Allegro*

However, the first Divertimento – or concerto as the autograph is headed – was not composed for Salzburg at all. The type of paper and the scoring for clarinets shows K113 to have been written in Milan, where Mozart had gone for the production of his *Ascanio in Alba*. It was probably the *starke Musik* which Leopold reported to have been played in the house of Herr von Mayer in November 1771. Did he mean by this 'strong music' that it was loud, or played by an orchestra rather than by a chamber group? The main interest is in Mozart's first use of the clarinet, though there is nothing here to indicate his later special love for the melancholy colour of the instrument. In Salzburg, where there were no clarinets, Mozart rescored the piece for oboes, cors anglais and bassoons, an unusually clumsy sound for him, but all very well in an open-air context.

K136, K137, K138 (125a, b, c) 3 Divertimenti in D, B flat and F

The autograph is headed 'Divertimento 1' in Mozart's own hand and 'Salzburg 1772 di W. A. Mozart', a dating we have no reason to doubt. It has been thought that these works were intended for string orchestra, perhaps as symphonies to take to Italy on his forthcoming journey, as Einstein suggested. The divertimenti sound marvellous when played by a chamber orchestra, and it is in this form that at least K136 has become one of Mozart's most popular works. But that is almost the only argument in favour of Einstein's supposition. Another argument is the plural indication *viole*, but that was a not uncommon writing error on Mozart's part. In the autograph of the String Quartet, K155 (134a), written in Italy that autumn, he himself corrected *viole* to *viola* and added *violoncello* above the word *basso*. In fact, the style of K136–K138 strongly resembles that of the Quartets K155–K160, except that in the latter the viola is given a little more independence. Other reasons for supposing them to be composed for quartet are the autograph heading 'divertimenti', and the fact that Mozart wrote no symphonies without wind instruments: if a dozen string players could be found, so apparently could two oboes and two horn players. Lastly, the bass part occasionally goes too low in the range of the double-bass, which of course plays an octave lower than written; composers did expect double-bass players to transpose up an octave automatically when this happened, but during this period Mozart nowhere else takes the double-bass part so low.

But all this is of merely historical interest. Why does this simple music of a sixteen-year-old give such perennial delight and perhaps move us as much, although in a different way, as an *adagio* by Beethoven? This question is much harder than those on points of musicology. In dealing with the most abstract of the arts, the writer on music has a particularly difficult task if he is not prepared to flounder in abstractions and adjectives. By examining K136 in a little more detail, we may at least indicate some directions for further consideration.

Let us look at the opening *allegro* of the Divertimento in D major, K136. First of all there is the sheer physical thrill produced by the élan of the motion, then the sweetness of the violins in thirds, the crossing of first and second violins high up with an excitement like the clash of swords, the grand gesture of the leap down to the G string, the wit and virtuosity of it all. It is perhaps the next best thing to 'driving briskly in a post-chaise with a pretty woman', which is how Dr Johnson would have spent his life had he had 'no duties, and no reference to futurity'. With a perfect sense of proportion Mozart leaves this brilliance half-way through the development for a totally different mood, conveyed by a calm, melancholy air in D minor in the first violins over pizzicato lower strings and an uneasy rustle by the second violins. He does this partly in order to give us, by way of contrast, a renewed sense of the sunshine in the opening when it returns.

What is most moving about the *andante* is its true simplicity, as so often found in Mozart's work. This is not the self-conscious beauty which insists on moving the listener, as is sometimes found in Mahler's music, nor the rather contrived 'simplicity' of some of Haydn's rustic slow movements, say that of the *Surprise* Symphony. Having only got as far as describing what this beauty is not, we may even be unable to separate it from its adjuncts, for some of the very features which appear to distinguish the young Mozart are to be found in the best of J. C. Bach's music (for example, the slow movements of the Op. 3 Symphonies).

Let us turn then to a close look at the finale, one of the happiest movements ever written. One reason for our pleasure in Mozart is in the mixture of the predictable and the surprising. The greatest pleasure given by a phrase in a composition or in a performance is surely occasioned by an initial surprise, to be instantly followed by an awareness of its rightness or even inevitability. Each musical phrase in the fifty-eight bars which make up the first part of the movement can be found in other works of Mozart's, and perhaps of his contemporaries (Ex. 17 overleaf). The melody is of that light folk-song type which Mozart often invoked, especially for his serenades and divertimenti. The second subject, for example, in bars 26-33, is ridiculously simple: like the noble Duke of York it marches up and marches down again. But one cannot help smiling, not condescendingly but with sheer happiness. Harmonically nothing very much happens. In fact, having written a fugato that never strays far from the tonic for the development section, Mozart remembers just in time to pull up on a B flat chord, followed by a diminished seventh, then A major, to ensure that feeling of homecoming which is the whole point of a recapitulation.

The interesting thing, and this is what really makes the movement, is Mozart's metrical skill. How does he use the cliché four-bar

Ex.17 K.136

Ex. 17 (cont.)

phrases which are the bricks of his structure? How does he avoid monotony and yet achieve classical balance? At this tempo one tends to think in eight-bar phrases, the natural length to consider as a simple group or to sing in one breath. And much of the movement is indeed made up of eight-bar phrases, each consisting of two identical or similar halves. Most of Mozart's contemporaries would have begun with bar 5 using bars 5–12 as the first melodic unit and 13–20 as the next; balanced enough but rather obvious. (Mozart actually does open his String Quartet, K160, with exactly the phrase in bars 5–8, but then answers it with no mere repetition but with something quite different.) Mozart's bars 1–4, apart from the cheeky flourish they provide, have the effect of making bars 5–8 the *second* half of an eight-bar phrase; so bars 9–12, instead of being a paler repetition of bars 5–8, begin a new eight-bar phrase of their own, a fact accentuated by the bass line going down an octave for greater intensity. Next, bars 9–12 are followed by bars 13–16 in another eight-bar group, and bars 17–20 are completed by the four-bar modulating phrase, bars 21–24. In one sense the half-phrase of bars 1–4 is finally balanced by the half-phrase of bars 21–24, while 5–12 and 13–20 can be thought of as symmetrical phrases, each made up of two almost identical halves. In another sense, we have the phrasing mentioned above – bars 1–8, 9–15, 16–24. This ambiguity helps to remove the feeling of a hurdle at the end of each phrase, a feeling present in much minor eighteenth-century music, and serves to ensure the onward flow of the music.

In the second subject we meet a similar piece of architecture. Bar 25 is an extra bar not belonging to any of its fellows. It is there firstly to establish the A – as things have happened so fast, we need a moment to realise that we have arrived in the dominant. Secondly, it provides a jolt out of any danger of excessive regularity in even the ambiguous eight-bar phrases mentioned above; and thirdly, we shall need it later on for structural purposes. Now come bars 26–29, exactly repeated in bars 30–33, and bars 34–37, exactly repeated in bars 38–41. But that is all the regularity we are allowed at a time, for bar 41 not only concludes the previous phrase but is clearly the first bar of a new six-bar phrase. So, once more we have the frisson of ambiguity and the flow which knocks down (or rather jumps over) hurdles. But what of the classical balance? Well, clearly the bar missing at bar 41 can be found in the extra bar, 25. And so the second subject has its sixteen bars after all. After this, with a semiquaver flourish by the first violin, the first part of the movement ends regularly enough with a further twelve bars.

Like the viewer of a picture the listener can take in the larger structure as well as the shape of the individual phrase; though this may be unconscious, it is this double sense, sometimes as here in unresolved contradiction, which gives particular satisfaction.

The Divertimento in B flat, K137, is equal in quality to K136, if not in popularity. It opens with the slow movement, a rare reference in Mozart to the old sonata *da chiesa*, as in his first String Quartet. The *allegro* has most of the brio of the first movement of K136 and the finale had much of the wit of its counterpart. The Divertimento in F major, K138, is rather stiff and formal compared to the others. Were it not for the evidence of the autograph, one would have guessed it to have been composed a good deal earlier, but of course Mozart might have copied it out from an earlier draft. The usual assumption that Mozart wrote everything straight down cannot be sustained. Many of Mozart's early works are wholly or partly in the hand of his father; these must have been copied from Mozart's own hasty scribbles, which were then thrown away.

K290 March   *K205 Divertimento in D*

1 *Largo – allegro*; 2 Menuetto; 3 *Adagio*; 4 Menuetto; 5 *Presto*

To judge from a reference in a letter of Leopold's, this music may have been written for performance at a garden party of Dr F. A. Mesmer in Vienna in August 1773. This famous practiser of hypnotism is mocked by Mozart and da Ponte in *Così fan tutte*, when the disguised Despina cures the poisoned lovers with a large magnet according to 'Mesmeric' principles. In K205 there is only one violin, and the bassoon is specified as a bass instrument, although this was usually taken for granted. The horns are left on their own on only two or three occasions – one expressive high horn passage comes in the opening *largo*. The *allegro*, like much of the Divertimento, has more Haydnish bustle and good spirits than really individual Mozartian flavour. The second half of the trio in the second movement has a drastic piece of writing that might have appealed to Haydn – the viola, given the tune for once, finds the violin following in canon one beat behind, treading on its heels in complete disregard of the harmony! The *adagio*, in a perfect piece of three-part writing, gives the violin and viola turns at playing and accompanying the long ornamental melody. The second minuet and trio are full of horn calls. The finale *presto* has an irrepressible subject which keeps bouncing back like a clown. The March is one of the most beautiful that Mozart wrote.

K248 March in F   K247 Divertimento in F

1 *Allegro*; 2 *Andante grazioso*; 3 Menuetto; 4 *Adagio*; 5 Menuetto; 6 *Andante – allegro assai*

This was composed for the name-day of Countess Antonia Lodron on 13 June 1776. We have already learned from Leopold's letters what happened to the poor Countess when Wolfgang had left Salzburg for Mannheim and Paris in 1778. Mozart took a good deal of trouble with this work – the Countess was a lady of consequence in Salzburg and many people would be listening to it. There is a one-page fragment of the Divertimento in F major, K288 (K246c), which he presumably abandoned for this work.

The first movement begins with a flourish to hush the chatter of the crowd (Mozart might have learned the necessity for this from his experience with the Divertimento K205 which opens *pianissimo*) and, when this is accomplished with good humour, allows a singing second subject to follow. We can follow the wit and imagination with which Mozart uses eighteenth-century form, disposing of his units of melody with a freedom not contained in the text books on sonata form. We have the opening flourish A (bars 1–4) beginning:

Ex.18

a second flourish B (bars 5–8), beginning:

Ex.19

and a comic commentary C (bars 9–12), beginning:

Ex.20

C returns almost like a rondo subject, for we meet it again in each half of the movement, to wind up the second subject, and also in the midst of the development. The recapitulation ignores A (Ex. 20) altogether, but Mozart closes the circle in the end, for an eight-bar coda brings us A C (Exx. 16 and 18). The second movement has a most beautiful melody of that yearning expression which has made the *andante* of *Eine kleine Nachtmusik* unforgettable: it is a simple rondo with varied returns. Even the minuets reveal how Mozart had by now found the way to make every phrase a personal, eloquent melody; none more so than the languid D minor trio introduced by the horns. The second minuet is more brisk and countrified with a *Ländler*. The *adagio* has the usual long decorated melody of the first violin, accompanied in triplets almost throughout. With his love of dramatic contrasts, Mozart is at pains to build up a solemn atmosphere in the slow march which introduces the finale, only to shatter this atmosphere with the arrival of the irrepressible rondo underlined by the horns in unison. It is full of delightful episodes, including the B flat one which predicts Beethoven's rage over the lost penny!

K287 (271b) Divertimento in B flat

1 *Allegro*; 2 Thema con 6 variazioni *andante grazioso*; 3 Menuetto; 4 *Adagio*; 5 Menuetto; 6 *Andante − molto allegro*

Mozart relates how he played this piece in a private concert in Munich, later in the year of its composition: 'Everybody looked astonished for I played as though I was the greatest violinist in Europe.' His father replied with good advice: 'I am not surprised that everyone was astonished, for you do not know how well you play the violin . . . . [when asked to play, always say] "I apologise in advance as I am no violinist," and then play brilliantly. That never fails.' K287 has one of the most virtuoso violin parts in Mozart's music, going right up to C three octaves above middle C. It also was composed for the Countess Lodron, for an indoor occasion in February 1777, and therefore did not require a march. It resembles K247 in construction, even to the point of withholding the recapitulation of the opening until the very end of the first movement, and mainly differs in the greater brilliance of the first violin part. Wolfgang must have been practising the violin energetically in the second half of 1776! The gavotte with variations has not the profundity of Mozart's later essays in the form. They are rather the beautifully made carvings around a rococo figure. Although the horns have their moment of glory in the third variation, and the fourth variation is based on canonic imitation between the viola and the first violin, it is in fact the first violin which dominates the proceedings. The *adagio* − based on the same pattern as the other *adagio*s in having a long cantilena over an accompaniment figure – has the most intricate ornamentation of a solo line to be found in Mozart's music. It could be used as a model for the idiomatic performances of eighteenth-century melodies. The minuets which flank the *adagio* have all the expressive qualities we noted in K247, with a minor trio for the first minuet, and broken octaves for the first violin in the trio of the more rustic second minuet.

In the finale, Mozart goes to even greater pains to create an amusing contrast than he had done in K247. An operatic recitative opens the scene: the first violin in the role of *opera seria* heroine appears to sing: 'O Dei, misera sono', and so on. Then in comes the most ridiculous little folk-tune 'D' Bäuerin hat d'Katz verlorn' (meaning that the farmer's wife has lost her cat, suitable matter for tragic lamentation). How the Salzburg audience must have laughed! The recitative returns once more before the coda, but that is only after a full rondo with a fireworks display on the first violin.

K445 March in D   K334 Divertimento in D

1 *Allegro*; 2 *Andante con 6 variazioni*; 3 Menuetto; 4 *Adagio*; 5 Menuetto; 6 Rondo, *allegro*

Written in the summer of 1779 for the patrician family of the Robinigs, K334 is the counterpart of the 'Post-horn' Serenade in being the only work of its kind composed after the great journey of 1777–9. But there is less difference between K334 and its predecessors than we have discovered in comparing the 'Haffner' and 'Post-horn' Serenades. The difference lies mainly in a closer approach to pure chamber music and in a richer harmonic palette. The opening, beginning *piano* on the upbeat to the third beat, is more subtle than the peremptory calls to attention of K247 and K287:

Ex.21

Although the first violinist requires considerable virtuosity (rising to Mozart's highest note yet, D three octaves and a tone above middle C), the other string parts have a greater share in the proceedings than in K287. In fact the opening subject appears even in the bass part: a belief that the double-bass would be too clumsy to play it led to doubts whether these works were really intended for double-bass rather than cello. On the other hand, by coming closer to the string quartet, Mozart virtually ignored the horns, which had contributed so much of the melodic character of the earlier divertimenti, especially in the finale of K205 and K247. They have a beautiful high *obbligato* part only in the fourth variation of the second movement; if they were capable of playing that, one wonders why Mozart did not use them more. Presumably because he was by now more interested in the pure string quartet; a surviving sketch K246b (320B) demonstrates the trouble he took in working out the counterpoint. Earlier on I lamented the harmonically static character of the serenades with their many minuet movements, especially when there were several trios in the tonic key – as in K131. Mozart clearly thought the same, for in the second menuetto, *Deutsche* with its characteristic snap (Ex. 22), his two trios are in the tonic minor and relative minor respectively.

Ex.22

Moreover, as in the 'Post-horn' Serenade, he adds a superb movement in D minor, the first of several variation movements in the minor and of similar melodic character (in the Violin Sonata K377, in the String Quartet K421, both in D minor, and the Variations for Piano and Violin in G minor K360). This is in every way a richer movement than the second movement of K287, where every variation had followed the harmonic shape of the theme. To take one subtle example in K334, the Neapolitan second which had been hinted at in the E flats towards the end of the theme is only fully, but then how gloriously, revealed in the fifth bar of the fifth variation with the *forte* E flat chord.

The third movement has one of Mozart's most seductive melodies, with that feminine swagger more often to be discovered in Boccherini than in Mozart. The ♩♩ ⅞ figure ensures a slow enough tempo. The *adagio* has again a long, decorated melody by the first violin. As in K247, Mozart uses the satisfying rhythm of even quavers against triplets, which gives something of the effect of a written-out rubato. The sixth movement could be the rondo finale of a concerto, both in its writing for the first violin and in its structure, the full sonata-rondo form, which he also used in the great piano concertos. It has melodic episodes that come but once, a second subject that returns as in first movement form, and the first rondo subject which is heard four times with all its repeats. Not that one could ever have too much of this exuberant, playful tune.

K522 'Ein musikalischer Spass'

1 *Allegro*; 2 Menuetto *meastra*; 3 *Adagio cantabile*; 4 *Presto*

The title 'A musical joke' appears in Mozart's thematic index; a possible explanation for the circumstances of its composition was offered on p. 10. Although two autograph copies of the second violin part of the first movement survive, one can hardly suppose that a string orchestra performed this joke; certainly the first violin must have been solo. Chamber music has been described as conversation between *civilised* people; in that case, K522 represents just the *ordinary* kind of conversation – somebody rambles on, others go off at a tangent, platitudes are repeated, discords are not resolved, relations are mostly false. The spoof was on bad composers, but the jokes are also at the expense of the performers. There are wrong notes on the horns in the menuetto, on the first violin in the *adagio* melody (the second note, F sharp, obviously does not really belong there and represents an out-of-tune F), and in the last three bars of the whole work – just in case anybody had failed to notice the joke – the four string instruments end in as many different keys. There are, however, many more jokes against composers: endless sequences, many bars of little more than vamping while waiting for the inspiration that never came, repeated ludicrous attempts at a fugato in the finale, which peters out before it has really begun, all sorts of pointless modulations and runs up and down, and gauche instrumental writing like absurd horn trills. The violin cadenza in the *adagio* is, ironically enough, the only cadenza for solo violin which has come down to us from Mozart: so at least we have his example of how not to do it! The opening of the finale is really rather attractive with its ten-bar theme – a Mozartian procedure to extend the expected eight bars by coming to a false close and needing two more bars to finish. Very rapidly we are jerked into remote keys (not entirely unlike Beethoven's procedure after the double-bar of some of his scherzos) and, equally abruptly, we are jerked back again. The trouble with K522 is that for much of the time Mozart is caricaturing the sheer tedium of some of his contemporaries' music: can one caricature tedium without, to some extent, invoking it?

K525 'Eine kleine Nachtmusik'

1 *Allegro*; 2 Romanze *andante*; 3 Menuetto *allegretto*; 4 Rondo *allegro*

Mozart cannot have been aware that this piece, titled with unconscious euphony, would become perhaps the best-known of all his works. It was composed while he was working on the second act of *Don Giovanni* (we know not for what occasion) and was noted down in his thematic index rather non-committally as a little serenade. This perennial popularity is undoubtedly justified, although there are many greater and deeper works. Mozart perfected his innate gift for balanced form in a phrase or, on a larger scale, in a movement, something which can be sensed even by those without musical training. There is not a note too many. Originally there were two minuets (they are mentioned in Mozart's index) but, like the second minuet of the 'Haffner' Symphony, one was lost. It is quite likely that Mozart himself removed it for the sake of the overall form. He had already decided on only one minuet for his last serenade, K388, and indeed he continued to be in two minds on the question whether a symphony needed a minuet or not, for even the later *Prague* Symphony does not have one. He was right to remove the second minuet of *Eine kleine Nachtmusik* for it would hardly have achieved its popularity if it had had to carry an extra minuet.

Even more important than the balance, of course, are the sheer sensuous glory of the sound and the tunes themselves. Mozart could write melodies of great simplicity, which are touching without sentimentality.

Although nearly always performed by an orchestra – and it sounds marvellous that way – there is little doubt that he wrote it for two violins, viola, cello and bass (the 'kleine' (little) surely implies that). We found that cellos did not take part in serenades, but here he specially noted 'bassi' in the plural, which seems to ask for the participation of a cello an octave above the double-bass, to fill in the wide gap between violas and double-bass occupied in the other divertimenti by the two horns.

The Music for Wind Band

If we ignore the marches and divertimenti referred to in Leopold's index as having been composed in 1767, but which have never been found, then Mozart's earliest works for wind band are two Divertimenti: that in B flat (K166), and that in E flat (K186). These were both for two oboes, two clarinets, two cors anglais, two horns and two bassoons, and were composed around March 1773 in, or certainly for, Milan (since Salzburg had no clarinets). The second bassoon only doubles the first; indeed there is a great deal of doubling in unison or in octaves, not easily avoided with this instrumentation, but occasionally producing a Wurlitzer effect.

Each Divertimento has an opening *allegro* (the one in K186 sounds like the oom-pa-pa accompaniment to a *Ländler*, but one has the uneasy feeling that whoever has 'got the tune' must have lost his place). After a sturdy menuetto, there is an *andante* in each Divertimento, and then an *adagio* which is certainly the high point in each work. Here the slow swing of the melody combines with sustained horns and high oboes to produce a sonority of great beauty, and to reveal, for the only time in these Divertimenti, the ear of the master. The finales are high-spirited contredanses in rondo form.

K187 (159c) Divertimento in C for two flutes, five trumpets and four timpani

Eight pieces taken from Gluck's *Paride ed Elena* and from ballets by Josef Starzer: the manuscript is in the hand of Leopold, but may have been a copy of Wolfgang's arrangement of these pieces. It must have been made for some festive open-air occasion about 1772.

K188 (240b) Divertimento in C for two flutes, five trumpets and three timpani

The manuscript of these six pieces is in the hand of Mozart, and none have been identified as copies from other sources. No one has very convincingly dated the composition (theories range from 1772 to 1777) since these simple little pieces – some only twenty bars in length – and the unique scoring give few points of contact with other compositions.

Somebody's idea of heaven, according to Sydney Smith, was 'eating *pâtés de foie gras* to the sound of trumpets'. Music at meals has certainly been the privilege and practice of all who could afford it from ancient times. In the eighteenth century it was provided for the nobility by wind-bands of liveried servants, invariably including pairs of bassoons and horns, and for the melody, pairs of oboes, clarinets and/or cors anglais. These bands were also heard to advantage in the open, where strings sound thin. Much of the music consisted of selections from recent operas; it was in this sort of way that tunes could achieve 'pop' status among opera lovers like Leporello, who can recognise recent 'hits' in Don Giovanni's *Tafelmusik*.

Mozart wrote five wind-divertimenti, almost certainly as *Tafelmusik* for the Prince Archbishop of Salzburg's band of two oboes, two horns and two bassoons.

K213 Divertimento in F (July 1775)
1 *Allegro spiritoso*; 2 *Andante*; 3 Menuetto; 4 Contredanse en rondeau *molto allegro*

K240 Divertimento in B flat (January 1776)
1 *Allegro*; 2 *Andante grazioso*; 3 Menuetto; 4 *Allegro*

K252 (240a) Divertimento in E flat (January 1776)
1 *Andante*; 2 Menuetto; 3 Polonaise *andante*; 4 *Presto assai*

K253 Divertimento in F (August 1776)
1 Thema con variazioni *andante*; 2 Menuetto; 3 *Allegro assai*

K270 Divertimento in B flat (January 1777)
1 *Allegro molto*; 2 *Andantino*; 3 Menuetto; 4 *Presto*

Mozart is at once the complete master of the form. The clumsy doubling of the Milan divertimenti has been left behind, and the music is in six independent parts, except where the bassoons join forces to provide a strong bass for the other four instruments. At the very beginning of K213 Mozart achieves the perfect blend of wit and grace – to the gruff *tutti* opening the first oboe replies in a cheeky *Till Eulenspiegel* way. There is as much variety as the medium can afford – K253 is one of only three of his works to open with variations; K252 has one of his three polonaises. The finales are brilliant contredanses or gigues.

K289 (K271g) Divertimento in E flat (spurious)

Of the wind divertimenti falsely attributed to Mozart those agreeable works KA226 and KA227 have been definitely dismissed into the pages of the spurious works by the sixth edition of the Köchel Catalogue and by almost everybody else, but the Divertimento in E flat, K289, must be discussed in detail, since it is rated as genuine by all the most respected authorities. No autograph has survived, and the pedigree of the earliest copies is uncertain, so its authenticity must stand or fall on the evidence of the music itself. From this one must conclude that it is the work of a not untalented contemporary and worth an occasional hearing, but definitely not by Mozart.

For a start, there is an odd lack of variety about the musical material, which is quite uncharacteristic of Mozart. The first movement is extraordinarily like the finale: it has the same sort of first subject with its excessive insistence on the key-note, the same rather lame attempts to escape by use of the flattened seventh, then, all attempts at modulation having failed, the same sudden switch to the dominant for a second subject of the same shape, and an almost identical coda theme, both movements concluding with a *diminuendo* on a pedal point. The melodic similarities between the openings (and other parts) of all four movements indicate poverty of invention rather than a deliberate imposition of unity: Mozart achieved the unity of a work by far more subtle means, and never repeated himself in this way. In the finale there are two serious mistakes of which Mozart would have been incapable – in the fourteenth and fifteenth bars of the development section there are parallel fifths between the treble and bass. Mozart very occasionally committed that musical solecism between the inner parts of his harmony, but he never did it as glaringly as this. The other mistake, or at least very clumsy piece of writing, is in the recapitulation of the second subject, where the second oboe is unable to play the accompaniment, previously a fifth higher, because it now goes below the range of the instrument. So it suddenly rises an octave to play above the melody line of the first oboe. Now, whenever Mozart ran into this kind of problem, usually that of going off the top of the piano's keyboard, he would solve it by some delightful variation, making a virtue of a necessity. K289 cannot therefore be by Mozart, but, for all that, it should not give less enjoyment than it has in the past. It has some very good things – the solemn *adagio* introduction, the Haydnesque menuetto and trio,

46

especially the beautiful *adagio* with its elaborate part for the first oboe, and the exhilarating finale.

THE THREE WIND SERENADES

K375 Serenade in E flat for two oboes, two clarinets, two horns and two bassoons

1 *Allegro maestoso*; 2 Menuetto; 3 *Adagio*; 4 Menuetto; 5 *Allegro*

On 3 November 1781 Mozart wrote to his father from Vienna:

At 11 o'clock last night I was serenaded by two clarinets, two horns and two bassoons playing my own music: I had written it for St Theresa's Day for the sister-in-law of Herr von Hickel, the court painter, where it was performed for the first time. The six musicians are poor wretches who play together quite nicely all the same, especially the first clarinettist and the two horn players. But my chief reason for writing it was to let Herr von Strack (a Gentleman of the Emperor's Bed Chamber), who goes there every day, hear something of mine. And so I composed a little bit reasonably. It was well received too and played in three different places on St Theresa's Night, because when they had finished it in one place they were taken somewhere else and paid to play it again. And so these musicians had the front gate opened for them, and when they had formed up in the yard, they gave me, just as I was about to undress for bed, the most delightful surprise in the world with the opening E flat chord.

Apart from the vivid picture it gives of a happy moment in Mozart's life, and the light it throws on the struggles of composers and performers, this passage dates the original sextet version of K375, which he modified in the following year by adding two oboes.

This occasional piece for poor itinerant musicians is not only the most difficult to play of all Mozart's music for wind instruments, but is the first wind piece of a greatness comparable to the string quartets. The structure of the first movement remains unique: five bars in Mozart's characteristic dotted E flat rhythm, followed by dissonances to heighten the tension, form a sort of introduction before the real *allegro* is unleashed in bar 25 (though the change of tempo is only apparent).

The second subject consists of no more than a few sighs from the oboe and clarinet (the serenading lover waiting in vain for some encouragement, as Hermann Abert, Mozart's greatest biographer, suggested). Only in the recapitulation do we hear the real second subject we have been waiting for, first played on the horn, then by the oboe and clarinet in octaves, the happiest tune imaginable. Things seem to be going better for the lover, but after a good deal of bubbling virtuosity the oboe sighs again just before the end. The first minuet is stately and formal with a very fine chromatic trio in C minor; the second minuet has a folk song-like melody and the lighter one-in-the-bar feeling of a German dance. (The first publication of the sextet version in 1804 included a second trio, which is not however in the autograph.) The *adagio* is also in E flat (K375 is the only major work with all the movements in the same key, unless we accept the Wind Sinfonia Concertante as authentic), an operatic ensemble of great beauty, in which the instruments take turns to sing the melody and to provide the repeated quaver accompaniment. The final rondo brings rustic merriment, allied to great virtuosity.

K388 (384a) Serenade in C minor for two oboes, two clarinets, two horns and two bassoons

1 *Allegro*; 2 *Andante*; 3 Menuetto; 4 *Allegro*

We do not know when and for whom the Serenade in C minor, K388, was composed. In a letter of 27 July 1782 to his father Mozart referred to a 'Nacht musique' he was writing for wind; this has been taken to be this serenade, but he was surely referring to his arrangement of *Die Entführung* which he mentioned in a letter a few days before. (This arrangement, if ever completed, has not turned up.) There is some thematic similarity between K388 and the opening of the Piano Sonata, K457, of October 1784, but the serenade must have been composed before the opening of the thematic catalogue in February 1784, since Mozart would hardly have forgotten to include it. Mozart himself later arranged it as a string quintet; indeed its musical quality justifies its inclusion in the most exalted company in all chamber music, whereas it is an exception among the Serenades in being in the minor mode and having only one minuet. But the original scoring is even more poignant.

After the formal opening of the *allegro*, bar 4 brings the falling diminished seventh (E flat to F sharp) which is to dominate the movement and indeed the whole work. Every note has its place in the architecture and emotional content of this great movement. Each new hearing will reveal new marvels; but listen especially to the development section, which begins so gently – only to be transformed by the oboe's cry in the fourteenth bar; and to that point which can always be counted upon for a special revelation in Mozart's movements in the minor – when in the recapitulation the second subject, heard before in the major, must undergo the tragic metamorphosis of the minor mode.

The *andante* provides a timely release from the tensions of the first movement. Mozart was to return to something very like this calm suave melody for the serenade 'Secondate, aurette amiche' in *Così fan tutte*. The movement is in sonata form with his customarily varied instrumentation in the recapitulation. The 'menuetto in canone' is no less fine than the minuet of the Symphony in G minor, sharing its rhythmic urgency with the accent on the third beat. It is also a perfect example of Mozart's use of academic means, canon, inverted canon and mirror canon, to a purely musical and emotional end. In the minuet the melody of the oboes in unison is repeated at one bar's distance an octave lower by the bassoons. The canon is not rigorously preserved throughout, but one is struck by the harshness of the harmony, with clashes of a second occurring in almost every bar. The trio is a double mirror canon, no more strict than that of the minuet, but proclaiming a breathless pastoral peace, or in imitation of the music the visual image of two swans reflected in still water (Ex. 23 overleaf).

The fourth movement is in the form of a theme with eight free variations. The fifth movement in the relative major (and introduced by the phrase which is to usher Donna Anna and Don Ottavio into the sextet in *Don Giovanni*) freely extends the length of the theme. The same heralding motif returns us to the minor for the sixth variation. The seventh consists of a simplified form of the theme, but over chromatic harmonies built on the diminished seventh that has played such an important role in the first and third movements. The final variation in C major is a last-minute tribute to the supposedly light-entertainment character of serenades.

K361 (370a) Serenade in B flat for two oboes, two clarinets, two basset-horns, two bassoons, four horns and double-bass

1 *Largo – Allegro molto*; 2 Menuetto with two trios; 3 *Adagio*; 4 Menuetto with two trios; 5 Romanze; 6 Thema con variazioni *andantino*; 7 Rondo *allegro molto*

On 23 March 1784 a Vienna newspaper announced that a coming benefit concert for Anton Stadler, the clarinettist, in the National Theatre would include 'a big wind piece of quite an exceptional kind composed by Herr Mozart'. A report published in Schink's *Literarische Fragmente* in 1785 speaks of the same event:

Ex.23 K.388

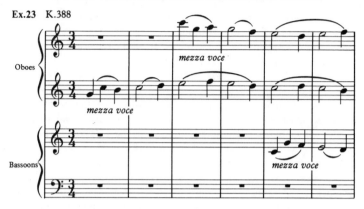

mezza voce

I heard music for wind instruments today by Herr Mozart, in four movements, glorious and sublime. It consisted of thirteen instruments; viz. four corni, two oboi, two fagotti, two clarinetti, two basset-corni, a contreviolin, and at each instrument sat a master – Oh what an effect it made – glorious and grand, excellent and sublime.

We can only conclude that K361, like K388, was written shortly before Mozart began his thematic index in February 1784. The traditional dating of 'Munich during the time of *Idomeneo* (1781)' has no factual basis.

Few composers matched Mozart's interest and skill in using instrumental colours. We know the impression the brilliant

Mannheim Orchestra had made on him in 1778. 'Oh, if only we had clarinets too,' he wrote wistfully to his father. 'You have no idea of the glorious effect of a symphony with flutes, oboes and clarinets.' In this Serenade (the autograph has the heading 'Grand Partita' in an unknown hand) Mozart was able to create the glorious effects of a lifetime. As well as two pairs of horns in different keys (to provide more notes, since they were not required, as they were in K375 and K388, to play anything but natural harmonics), and his favourite clarinettist, Stadler, to lead, Mozart used two basset-horns. It was only in the last six or seven years of his life that he really developed his writing for clarinets and basset-horns, though Leopold had mentioned some compositions for basset-horns amongst other instruments in the 1767 list of his son's works. Their plaintive tones – Bernard Shaw spoke of their 'watery melancholy' – became a characteristic sound in his last years. The contrabass instrument was the string double-bass, though it is possible that Mozart would have used a contra-bassoon if a good player could have been found.

Only four movements were played at the première. The manuscript implies that all seven movements were written at the same time but there may have been practical considerations of time available for rehearsal or performance. (Incidentally, Mozart could not have been present since he was himself performing in his subscription concert at the Trattnerhof that evening.) In the first movement the formal introduction builds up a climax on the chord of the ninth and goes out in the sighs of oboes and clarinets. The *allegro molto*'s subject has the snappy witty character of comic opera (it is in fact the theme of an aria in Philidor's *Maréchal ferrant*, 'Je suis douce, je suis bonne', which Mozart might have heard in Paris); it also serves, with a melodic extension, as second subject, a procedure far rarer with Mozart than with Haydn, but we are compensated for this economy with a new tune at the start of the development. There is a delightful preparation for the recapitulation, in which the opening phrase is echoed by various instruments in various keys until we find ourselves at home again almost without realising it. At the end a coda follows a whole bar's rest – hesitating between soulful utterance and the jolly military manner customary in a large assembly of wind instruments.

In the second movement the menuetto is once again based on Mozart's mastery of contrasts: the stately opening *forte* is answered *piano* by the pleading oboe, and each section is rounded off by the clarinet's gentle valediction. In the second section there is a canon between treble and bass on a horn pedal note, a marvellous effect which seems to suspend time. The first trio is in E flat major but with the dark colour of clarinets and basset-horns. The second trio is a truly Mozartian mixture of merry wind triplets and melancholy G minor expression, the conclusion of each half being particularly beautiful – each time the horn call in the major is answered by oboes and basset-horns shaking their heads and returning to the minor.

The *adagio* of the third movement is the loveliest of all movements written for wind instruments. It is a terzetto with all the dignity of expression of the Greek heroes of *Idomeneo*, in which the voice parts are sung by the first oboe, first clarinet and first basset-horn. The other instruments (there are only two horns) provide an accompaniment on a rhythmical figure which is unvaried for forty-one out of the forty-six bars – with an effect not of monotony but of incantation. Small wonder that somebody turned the movement into a religious chorus, *Quis te comprehendet*, once attributed to Mozart. The basset-horn has some leaps of over two octaves, so characteristic of Mozart's vocal music.

As in the other minuet, the merry *forte* staccato statement in the fourth movement is answered by a soft legato. The first trio, in the rare key of B flat minor, is dominated by the wistful basset-horns, the second is a swirling *Ländler* in which the unison of oboe, basset-horn and bassoon provides rustic colour.

The fifth movement is headed 'Romanze', a term Mozart used only five times in heading an instrumental piece. Did he mean anything special: for instance, that the melody was taken from a song? If he did, the songs have never been discovered. Perhaps he just meant a simple and expressive tune. There was usually a *minore* section in the middle. So there is here: the noble E flat *adagio* song gives way to the dark, impatient *allegretto* in C minor.

The music of the sixth movement is practically identical with the second movement of the Flute Quartet in C major (KA171), supposedly written in 1778 and, at least, almost certainly before K361. It is therefore amazing how aptly it is scored in these six variations, the last of which is a *Ländler* with a coda.

After the many moods of the Serenade, Mozart ends cheerfully with the seventh movement. The doubling of oboe and clarinet in the rondo theme make it hard to keep out thoughts of military bands, but one must submit to the delightful brilliance of all the instruments playing in turn and together.

KA229 (4396) 5 Divertimenti in B flat

Among the many letters which Mozart's widow wrote to music publishers to offer unpublished manuscripts for sale is one to André of Offenbach, dated 31 May 1800, in which she says: 'One ought to speak to the clarinettist Stadler senior about such things. He had ... copies of unknown trios for basset-horns. He claims that the trunk containing them was stolen from him, but others assure me that it was pawned for 73 ducats.' Then a little further down she lists: 'Score of three basset-horns, five numbers. The voice parts of these notturni by Jacquin are already with the publisher Traeg amongst others, but I do not think they are out yet.'

These Notturni for two sopranos and bass with an accompaniment of two clarinets and basset-horn, or in some cases three basset-horns, were composed (with the help of Mozart's host, it seems) for social evenings at the house of his friend Gottfried von Jacquin, though only one was ever entered in Mozart's thematic catalogue, on 16 July 1788. It is generally supposed that the Divertimenti were written for the same occasions. No autograph survives, and indeed even the instrumentation is uncertain. They were published in the early years of the nineteenth century for two basset-horns and bassoon, and for two clarinets and bassoon (with two horns ad lib.). There is, however, a strong argument to suggest that the original scoring was for three basset-horns, the third being generally an octave higher than the usual published bassoon part. (The autograph does survive of an *adagio*, K410 (484d) for two basset-horns and bassoon, but there is also the Adagio, K411 (K484a) for two clarinets and three basset-horns.) At all events, the Divertimenti must have been written, like most of Mozart's late clarinet and basset-horn music, for his brilliant – if dissolute – friend Anton Stadler; Constanze Mozart clearly had not changed her mind about him with the passage of years!

The Divertimenti are all in B flat – in fact all the movements are, except for one polonaise and the trios of the minuets, which are in the tonic minor, dominant or subdominant. The first four Divertimenti are of the normal construction: *allegro*, minuet, *adagio*, minuet, rondo; but the fifth seems to be a collection of disconnected pieces: *adagio*, minuet, *adagio*, *andante* (romance), polonaise. (A sixth Divertimento, published in the original editions, consists of arrangements of arias from *Figaro* and *Don Giovanni*: it was soon dismissed as spurious.)

These are well-made little pieces with, at times, an affecting autumnal quality, the result of the instrumental colour and the simple elegiac character of the melodies. However, taken more than a little at a time, they might well prove monotonous – unless it were as a background to supper in a garden, the circumstances which probably gave rise to them.

Mozart's Music for Dancing

'Madame Mozart told me that great as his genius was, he was an enthusiast in dancing, and often said that his taste lay in that art rather than in music.' Thus Michael Kelly, the first Don Basilio. Throughout Mozart's life there are references to his love of dancing. He was said to have had lessons from the great Vestris (who once declared that the century had only produced three great men, Frederick the Great, Voltaire and a third whom modesty would not permit him to name). Schiedenhofen's diary mentions the twenty-year-old Mozart at a fancy-dress ball dressed as a barber's apprentice. In Vienna in January 1783 Mozart himself gave a ball, entrance two guilders per gentleman – 'We began at six in the evening and finished at seven – what? only one hour? No, no, at seven in the morning!' He asked his father to forward his Harlequin costume, and in March 1783 he took part in a masquerade in the Redenthensaal – 'I composed the scenario and the music, the dancing master kindly controlled our steps, and I must tell you we really played quite well!' The last account of Mozart's dancing is by Joseph Deiner, who saw him dancing in his room with his wife in the winter of 1790 to keep warm, for he had no money for firewood.

The rhythms of the dance are everywhere to be heard in Mozart's music, and not only in the movements specifically headed 'minuet' etc. In both *Figaro* and *Don Giovanni* the dances are essential to the plot. When Count Rosenberg, Director of Vienna's theatres, censored the ball scene in *Figaro* on the grounds that 'it displeased the Emperor to see dances in his theatre', Mozart in despair threatened to rush to the Emperor and withdraw the whole opera. His librettist, da Ponte, very much the hero of the autobiography in which he relates this, used devious means to make Rosenberg confess to the Emperor that he had tried to cut out this scene to avoid having to hire dancers from other theatres.

Mozart wrote several dozen contredanses and German dances and well over a hundred minuets. The minuet was the dance of the court. Only one couple danced it at a time, beginning and ending by bowing to the Presence, then moving unhurriedly through a set of figures and hardly even touching hands. The steps reveal that the minuet is best thought of in two-bar phrases (which must have some bearing on the performance of the music), for they occur on the first, third, fourth and fifth beats, while the dancers paused and bent the supporting knee on the second and sixth beats. The German dance or *Deutsche* came from the *Ländler* (which means country dance) and was the ancestor of the waltz, which was soon to sweep all before it. The contredanse, the name being apparently derived from the English country dance, was a group dance with set figures like the later lancers and quadrille.

THE SALZBURG DANCES, 1769–77

K65a (61b)   *7 Minuets* for strings (January 1769)
K61g   *2 Minuets* (fragmentary, 1769)
K122 (73t)   *Minuet in E flat* (Bologna, August 1770)
K123 (73g)   *Contredanse in B flat* (Rome, April 1770)
K104 (61e)   *6 Minuets* ⎫
K105 (61f)   *6 Minuets* ⎬   (1769–72, at least partially copied from Michael Haydn)
K164 (130a)   *6 Minuets* ⎭
K61h   *6 Minuets* (1769–72)
K103 (61d)   *19 Minuets* (1769–72)
K176   *16 Minuets* (December 1773)
K363   *3 Minuets without trios* (1774-6 or later)
K101 (250a)   *4 Contredanses* (1776, probably partially by Leopold Mozart)
K267 (271c)   *4 Contredanses* (February 1777)
K269b   *Contredanses* for Count Czernin (January 1777, piano score only)
K315a (315g)   *8 Minuets* (February 1779, piano score only)

Most of this music was written for the Salzburg carnivals, the seasons of feasting and riot which precede Lent. In 1779 the Archbishop of

Salzburg had to forbid harlequinades during processions. Maria Theresa had forbidden all masked balls in her vast territories, except under police supervision, for why should law-abiding persons wear masks at all? Joseph II restored them, for no one enjoyed them more than he. Dancing was popular in Austria long before Mozart and remains so today, but it is with the arrival of the waltz at this time that this popularity gradually led to the veritable mania which culminated in the period of Johann Strauss, father and son. Even in Mozart's day, however, the people of Vienna were dancing mad, wrote Michael Kelly.

As the carnival approached, gaiety began to display itself on all sides; and when it really came nothing could exceed its brilliancy. The ridotto rooms, where all the masquerades took place, were in the palace [ie the Redoutensäle]; and spacious and commodious as they were, they were actually crammed with masqueraders. I never saw, or indeed heard of any suite of rooms, where elegance and convenience were more considered; for the propensity of the Viennese ladies for dancing and going to carnival masquerades was so determined, that nothing was permitted to interfere with their enjoyment of their favourite amusement – nay, so notorious was it, that for the sake of ladies in the family way, who could not be persuaded to stay at home, there were apartments prepared, with every convenience for their accouchement, should they be unfortunately required .... The ladies of Vienna are particularly celebrated for their grace and movements in waltzing, of which they never tire. For my own part I thought waltzing from ten at night until seven in the morning, a continual whirligig, most tiresome to the eye and ear, to say nothing of any worse consequences...

After this suggestion of gay abandon, Mozart's dances will strike a dignified note. In the early dances the strings play the essential parts and the wind only add colour, a colour, however, which is often the salt and pepper of the music. The first set of all was written for strings only (two violins and bass – none of the dance music has violas) the day before Mozart's thirteenth birthday, and is one of the few that can be dated with certainty. It is composed with delightful melodic invention and a rhythmic freedom which is later gradually abandoned. Here he often goes beyond the standard eight-bar section; later he only occasionally added to this section two bars of an echo effect, while the great Vienna dances are entirely constructed of eight-bar sections. The fourteen-year-old Mozart sent the Contredanse, K123, home from Rome. His father adds:

He requests Herr Cirillus Hoffmann to compose the steps to it in such a way that when the two violins play as leaders only one pair of dancers should dance, and when the whole band comes in with all the instruments the whole company should dance together. It would be best if five pairs would dance it, the first pair beginning the first solo, the second pair the second and so on, since there are five solos and five *tutti*s.

K123 is a tiny jewel of slightly over a minute's duration, a sort of child's view of Handel, utterly disarming in its innocence. It is characteristic of Mozart that he saw the dances as well as hearing the music in his mind.

Several of the early minuets, such as the first two of K104, are identical with some of Michael Haydn's. Though it is dangerous to speak of copies and influences when one lacks the relative dates of composition, there seems little doubt that Mozart was the plagiarist: he reveals his interest, if not his admiration, when he writes to his sister in 1770, 'Write to me how you like the Haydn minuets, if they are better than the first ones'. One wonders why he bothered to copy them at all, when he could probably have composed some of his own in about the same time. For the speed of his work is apparent in the delightful and clearly original K103 set, where one notices at least four cases of parallel fifths, errors of musical grammar rare in Mozart. But the minuets of K104, K105 and K164 do not carry the marks of Mozart's inspiration: further research may well reveal more Michael Haydn originals.

THE VIENNA DANCES, 1782–4

K106 (588a)	*Overture and 3 Contredanses*
K461 (448a)	*5 Minuets*
K462 (448b)	*6 Contredanses*
K463 (448c)	*2 Minuets with alternating Contredanses*
K409 (383f)	*Minuet in C*

The Minuet in C, K409, was neither composed for dancing nor for inclusion in a symphony, its eighty-nine bars making it much too long for either function. It was probably an entr'acte in one of Mozart's concerts, like two of the Marches, K408. It is a work of great beauty, the formal opening giving way to chamber-music delicacy and melting suspensions in the second section; the trio is a concertante for flute and oboe. K461 was planned as a set of six, but the last minuet remained a fragment of eight bars. K462 was originally written for strings only, the wind being added on a separate sheet, but in K461 the wind is beginning to assert its independence in a small way – for example, the bassoon no longer moves inevitably with the bass but sometimes in octaves with the violins or even independently. There are also some thrilling contributions by high horns. K463, later headed 'Two Quadrilles' by Nissen, is one of the most enjoyable of all the sets, its wistful slow minuets alternating with jolly contredanses.

All the dating is conjectural. To give an example of the problem of dating Mozart's music – Köchel put K106 into 1770 and Einstein suggested 1790–1. K106 No. 1 does resemble K603 No. 1 of 1791, but why did not Mozart put K106 in his thematic index? Of course, he might have simply overlooked it at a busy time; on the other hand the violin figures of the tiny overture of K106 recall the Marches, K408, of 1782, and the most likely dating is just before the beginning of the thematic index in February 1784. The same sort of argument applies to K461, K462 and K463, but thematic similarities are sometimes bewildering. For example, the second section of K462 No. 5 is almost identical with that of the finale of the Divertimento K186 of 1773. But then the finale of the Serenade K361 borrows a tune Mozart had used in the Clavier Duet Sonata which he wrote at the age of nine. The hunting of melodic similarities, though very interesting in the vocal music where one finds, for example, certain moods repeatedly expressed by certain intervals, is less a reliable tool for musicology than a stimulating entertainment!

SIX GERMAN DANCES, 1787

In January 1787 Mozart paid his first visit to Prague. For the first time since his childhood he was able to bask in his own fame, writing home that 'nothing is played, blown, sung or whistled except *Figaro*!' He wanted to do nothing but enjoy himself at balls and concerts, though he did accept a commission to write an opera for the Italian Company: this turned out to be *Don Giovanni*. Count Johann Pachta tricked him into writing at least one work which can be dated precisely. It was written on 6 February 1787.

We invited him at least one hour before the other guests; when Mozart arrived punctually on pleasure bent, he was led into a study and served not dinner but pen, ink and paper. By the time the other guests had arrived, he had composed the six 'Tedeschi' [K509].

So goes the tale, recounted by Nissen, but could even Mozart have written out, let alone composed, twenty-two pages of music in an hour? Since there is a *da capo* for each dance *and* its trio, the total duration is twelve minutes. The brilliant scoring includes piccolo and trumpets. Alone among his German dances, except for the *Teitsch* at Don Giovanni's ball, these dances are noted in 3/8 time, though this probably has no significance. More important, this is the only set of dances that plays continuously: after the six varied and exuberant, if not particularly profound, dances excitement mounts in the whirling coda. This set can be considered as the ancestor of a whole century of waltzes by the Strausses and others: and it is, by virtue of its continuity, the most suitable for inclusion in concert performances.

THE REDOUTENSAAL DANCES, 1788–91

(Dates from Mozart's thematic index)

K534	Contredanse 'Das Donnerwetter' (survives in piano score only)	14 January 1788
K535	Contredanse 'La Bataille'	23 January 1788
K535a	3 Contredanses (survives in a piano score only)	Early 1788
K536	6 German dances	27 January 1788
K565	2 Contredances (lost)	30 October 1788
K567	6 German dances	6 December 1788
K568	12 Minuets	24 December 1788
K571	6 German dances	21 February 1789
K585	12 Minuets	December 1789
K586	12 German dances	December 1789
K587	Contredanse 'Der Sieg vom Helden Coburg'	December 1789
K599	6 Minuets	23 January 1791
K600	6 German dances	23 January 1791
K601	4 Minuets	5 February 1791
K602	4 German dances	5 February 1791
K603	2 Contredanses	5 February 1791
K604	2 Minuets	12 February 1791
K605	3 German dances ('Sleigh Ride')	12 February 1791
K606	6 *Ländler* (survives in version for strings only)	28 February 1791
K607 (605a)	Contredanse 'Il trionfo delle donne' (fragment)	28 February 1791
K609	5 Contredanses ('Non più andrai')	6 March 1791
K610	Contredanse 'Les filles malicieuses' (as K609 No. 5, plus flute and 2 horns)	6 March 1791
K611	Contredanse 'Hurdy-gurdy' (identical with K602 No. 3)	6 March 1791

After 1781, when he was stormily dismissed from the service of the Prince Archbishop of Salzburg, until the end of his life ten years later, Mozart had no permanent employment. His poverty, which cannot altogether be blamed on his and Constanze's spendthrift ways, seems to show that the time was not yet ripe for an independent composer, such as Beethoven managed to be – more or less successfully. Indeed Mozart always hoped for a post. The young Archduke, who had been impressed by *Ascanio in Alba* in Milan in 1777, received this letter from his mother, the Empress:

You ask if you may take the young Salzburger into your service. I do not know why you should, for I do not believe that you are in need of composers or other useless people. If it gives you pleasure, however, I do not wish to stand in your way.

(There are no prizes for guessing if Mozart got the job!)

The years 1784–6 saw the high point of Mozart's worldly success. He had begun the series of piano concertos, which had at first fascinated the Viennese audience, with K449 in February 1784, and it was surely this success which induced him to open his thematic catalogue with that work. Leopold Mozart visited Vienna the following winter and described Wolfgang's triumphs in a letter to his daughter. Everything seemed to be going well and one would have thought that *Figaro* in 1786 would have assured Mozart of a prosperous life in Vienna. But it was precisely at this point that the fickleness of the public, or rather the fact that his music required too much rehearsal by the musicians and too much concentration for the audience, began to leave his concerts ill-attended and the sub-scription lists for compositions he proposed to publish almost empty. The popularity of his music in Prague, which gave rise to the commission for *Don Giovanni*, offered new hopes; and there might have been chances in Prussia or England – but Mozart could hardly have supposed that he would be in a better position there than in the Imperial capital of Vienna, where he was known to the Emperor and all the nobility! Surely an official position with an adequate salary was not an unreasonable hope.

At last, on 7 December 1787, he received the title of *Kammerkompositeur* (Imperial Chamber Composer) from the 'liberal' Joseph II. Alas, the Emperor's 'liberality' was confined to his politics: Rochilitz recalled some ten years later that the 800 guilders salary Mozart was paid was just enough to pay the rent. Mozart is said to have described it as 'too much for what I do, too little for what I could do'. The only compositions connected with his official duties were the dances for the Redoutensaal, though they were not perhaps directly demanded from him in his court capacity. The Redoutensaal, still part of the Imperial Palace in Vienna, was the scene of many balls in the carnival season, patronised by the Emperor but attended by people of all classes. Haydn and Beethoven – among others – provided the music, and Mozart's last twenty sets of dances were composed for them. Since the orchestra was composed of the same excellent players as that of the National Theatre next door, for whom Mozart composed *Figaro* and *Così fan tutte*, we can share in the delight he took in their virtuosity. For the sake of the dancers, all the music had to be in eight-bar phrases, an almost crippling limitation when we consider how Mozart, of all composers, varied his classical symmetry by dropping or adding a bar or two – one of the marks which distinguish him from his minor contemporaries.

But he had several other ways of achieving variety, the chief of which was in the scoring, the most colourful of any of his music. In K536 he still does not go beyond using the flutes and bassoons in octaves with the violins, but by K568 we meet the full glory of his orchestration. There are duets and trios for flute, oboe and bassoon (the trios of K568 No. 9 and K599 No. 4); there are important solos for flute, clarinet and even horn; there is the occasional intervention of percussion; and there is that most Mozartian procedure of juxtaposing the whole group of the strings against the wind, so that, though either would make a satisfactory whole, the combination of the two produces a marvellous richness of orchestration and counterpoint.

Ex.24   K.599

Ex. 24 (cont.)

Another means of variety is in the rhythmic freedom Mozart found in Bohemia – for example, the openings of K567 No. 1 (Ex. 25) and K585 No. 5 (Ex. 26).

Ex.25   K.567

Ex.26   K.585

These sound as though they were written in 2/4 time. There is a Spanish fandango rhythm in the trio of K568 No. 6. These short dances do not give much scope for harmonic adventures, but we do find, for example, this unusually drastic scheme, which Mozart would not have used in his serious compositions:

Ex.27 K.571

Some of the trios in the minor have an exotic character:

Ex.28 K.571

And on one occasion there is a wonderful Schubertian melancholy (Ex. 29 overleaf). The sets of German dances usually end with a coda, dominated by the piccolo, a wild gallop, *crescendo* and *accelerando*.

There are also the descriptive or 'effects' pieces: the contredanses 'La Bataille' and 'Victory of the Hero Coburg', concerning the current campaigns against the Turks (Mozart took rather a toy-soldier view of the wars which bedevilled Europe throughout his life); the 'Thunderstorm', and the Canarybird in K600 No. 5; the musical references, to *Figaro* in K609 and to other operas in K607 and

Ex.29 K.571

K610; and the unusual instruments, the hurdy-gurdy in K601 No. 2 and K602 No. 3, the sleigh-bells and post-horns of K605 No. 3. K567–K599 constitute the high point of musical invention and orchestration. One might say that he was experimenting in the relatively unimportant medium of dance music with a view to the symphonies he hoped to write in 1792. From K600 onwards (and these are rather unjustly the most often played of his dances) he falls into the popular Viennese simplicity, which was to contribute so much to the *Magic Flute*.

THE BALLET MUSIC

KA207

The lost ballet for *Ascanio in Alba*, 1777, may be contained in the nine Clavier pieces (KV⁶c 27.06) (see Mozart Jahrbuch 1964).

KA109 (135a)

Sketches in Mozart's hand to a ballet, *Le gelosie del seraglio*, but since seven of the pieces have been identified as being Starzer, this may be a notation of music heard.

K299c
Sketches for a ballet, probably *Les petits riens*, Paris 1778.

K299b (KA10)
Ballet *Les petits riens* Paris 1778. A gavotte in B flat, K300, and KA103 (320f) a fragmentary contredanse *La Chasse* may be drafts for K299b.

K367
Ballet for *Idomeneo*, Munich, January 1781.

K446 (416d)
Music to a pantomime, Vienna February-March 1783, in which Mozart himself danced the part of Harlequin. Incomplete first violin part only.

Considering his devotion to the dance, it is a pity that Mozart never wrote a major ballet – a sort of *Figaro* of the dance, which would have changed the history of the art. If only Jean Georges Noverre's hopes, expressed in his *Letters on the Dance* of 1760, had been realised in a Mozartian masterpiece. The rather trivial ballets he did compose – not that the *music* of the *Idomeneo* ballet is trivial – are of the very kind Noverre had chuckled over so grimly:

The ballet master will receive a violin part in which is to be read: '*Passepied* for games and jokes, *Gavotte* of the Cupids, *Tambourin* and *Rigadoun* of the shepherds, *Staccato* of the devils, entry of the Greeks and *Chaconne*' – here he has his instructions, let him carry out this magnificent and profound programme as best he may!

Mozart's orchestral works for Paris in 1778 had an unfortunate fate on the whole. Some were lost altogether and some turned up a century later in a garbled form, like the Sinfonia Concertante for Wind and the ballet *Les petits riens*. Mozart had often dined with Noverre, in Paris, and hoped to get a commission for a big opera in the French style through him. On 9 July 1778 he gives his father the sad report on his mother's death, going on a little later

about Noverre's ballet I only wrote that he *might* produce a new one – well, he only needed half a ballet and I wrote the music for it – that is to say six pieces in it would be by others, they consist of a lot of miserable old French airs, the symphony and the contredanse, twelve pieces in all would be by me.

This ballet has already been done four times with great applause, but I shall write nothing more now unless I know in advance what I am to get for it, for this was written only to do Noverre a friendly service.

The first performance was at the Grand Opéra at the conclusion of Piccinni's *Le finte gemelle* on 11 June. Mozart's name appeared nowhere. Next day the *Journal de Paris* described the contents:

It consists of three scenes forming separate and almost detached episodes. The first is purely anacreontic: it shows Cupid ensnared and put into a cage, a most agreeable choreography. In it Mme Guimard and M. Vestris the Younger employ all the grace and skill the subject allows. The second is a game of blind-man's buff: M. d'Auberval whose talent so pleases the public, plays the principal part here. The third is a mischievous prank of Cupid's; he introduces a shepherdess disguised as a shepherd to two other shepherdesses, who fall in love with the supposed shepherd, who, to undeceive them, finally uncovers her bosom. This scene is made very piquant by the grace and intelligence of the three dancers. We should add that at the moment Mlle Asselin disabuses the two shepherdesses, several voices cried 'bis'. The variations which concluded the dancing were much applauded!

The music, as it has come down to us, appears to be by three composers: Mozart, an unknown competent composer, and an unknown incompetent one. Mozart's overture makes the smallest demand on its public: it actually sets something of a record by never leaving the tonic key at all. It is difficult to find a further eleven pieces worthy of Mozart even when he is putting on his most sugared manner for the occasion, but one could accept the *andantino* with the off-stage flute (No. 9), the *larghetto* (No. 11), the gavotte (No. 12) quoting the same Czech carol as the finale of the Seventh Violin Concerto (but since that is also a work of unproved authorship, it is in no position to confer authenticity on the gavotte), the gigue (No. 14), delightful if not characteristic of Mozart, the *gavotte gracieuse* (No. 15), the best piece of the ballet, the winsome pantomine (No. 16), the expressive *legato* gavotte (No. 18), and perhaps also the concluding slow march (No. 19) but for its dubious wind writing.

The period of the composition and production of *Idomeneo*, two and a half years later, was one of the happiest in Mozart's life. All the same, he wrote on 19 December 1780, 'One cannot but be happy to be finally freed of such a laborious task', adding on 30 December, 'Afterwards I shall have the honour of writing a divertissement for the opera, for there is to be no separate ballet', and lastly on 18 January, 'Till now I've been kept busy with those cursed dances – *Laus Deo* – I have survived it all!' The première was on 29 January

1781 in the Elector's new opera house (later called the *Residenztheater*). The ballet-master was M. Le Grand. The dances may have been performed at the end of Act I or at the end of the opera, but presumably rather as a formal divertissement than with a scenario that had any connection with the opera. These divertissements provided the customary conclusion of French operas, including those of Gluck, whose influence is never stronger on Mozart than here, the subject of the opening chaconne being taken straight from that in *Iphigénie en Aulide*.

The chaconne, together with the dances which are joined to it, forms an immense and powerful rondo, Mozart's longest instrumental movement. The chief of its many moods is one of brilliant pomp. As in his earliest ballet, the contredanse K123 of 1770, Mozart visualised the dances: from his indications in the score, we learn that the entire corps de ballet danced at each return of the rondo theme of the chaconne and in the concluding *più allegro*, while the intervening episodes were a 'Pas seul de Mad. Falgera', a 'Pas de deux de Mad. Hartig et Mr. Antoine' and so on, the best and longest spot being kept for Mr Le Grand himself.

The passacaille is another rondo, a little less sumptuous than the chaconne and without trumpets and drums. The little *passepied en rondeau* for Mlle Redwen is only scored for strings and oboes and of a touching simplicity. The evergreen melody of the gavotte came into Mozart's head again when he wrote the finale of the Piano Concerto, K503 in 1786. The *ancien régime* seems to dance out to its nostalgic strains.

Index